December, 1998

To Lottie
With...
your loving care.
May 1999 bring peace
of mind & happiness your way.
With love,
Marianne

Bread and Roses
DOROTHY INGLIS

Bread and Roses
DOROTHY INGLIS

St. John's, Newfoundland
1996

©1996, Dorothy Inglis

Appreciation is expressed to *The Canada Council* for publication assistance.

The publisher acknowledges the financial contribution of the *Department of Tourism and Culture, Government of Newfoundland and Labrador*, which has helped make this publication possible.

All rights reserved. No part of this work covered by the copyrights hereon may be reproduced or used in any form or by any means—graphic, electronic or mechanical—without the prior written permission of the publisher. Any requests for photocopying, recording, taping or information storage and retrieval systems of any part of this book shall be directed in writing to the Canadian Reprography Collective, 214 King Street West, Suite 312, Toronto, Ontario M5H 2S6.

∝ Printed on acid-free paper

Cover design: Janice Udell

Published by
KILLICK PRESS
an imprint of CREATIVE BOOK PUBLISHING
a division of 10366 Newfoundland Limited
a Robinson-Blackmore Printing & Publishing associated company
P.O. Box 8660, St. John's, Newfoundland A1B 3T7

Printed in Canada by:
ROBINSON-BLACKMORE PRINTING & PUBLISHING

Canadian Cataloguing in Publication Data

Inglis, Dorothy, 1926–

  Bread and roses

  ISBN 1-895387-68-X

  1. Women — Canada   2. Feminism — Canada.   I. Title.

HQ1453.I53   1996   305.42'0971   C96-950039-4

To Gordon, husband and editor, who always understood.

And to Gord, Bill and Mary whose lives so enriched ours.

Table of Contents

Preface: How this all started ix

Chapter 1:   The Way We Were 1

Chapter 2:   Women's Place 13

Chapter 3:   Charge of the Right Brigade 25

Chapter 4:   The Protection Racket 35

Chapter 5:   Vive la Difference 47

Chapter 6:   Family Matters 59

Chapter 7:   Eternal Vigilance 75

Chapter 8:   As the Stomach Turns 89

Chapter 9:   Some of My Best Friends 99

Chapter 10: And We Thought We'd Got Rid of Brian 109

Chapter 11: Suffer the Little Children 121

Chapter 12: Whose Country is it Anyway? 131

Chapter 13: War and Women 139

Chapter 14: A Planet Worth Saving 145

Appendix: Some publications and organizations
             I have quoted or mentioned 153

Overheard at the Newfoundland Provincial Women's Lobby, held with Members of the House of Assembly, April 1991:

> One male reporter: How can you tell which ones are the feminists?
>
> Second male reporter: That's easy, b'y. They're the ones with sensible shoes and crazy earrings.

How this all Started

A colleague once told my husband that he had felt obliged to come to my defence. Friends of his had been commiserating with him over the ordeal of working on a public committee with such a hardline feminist as Dorothy Inglis. To their surprise he had assured them that it wasn't so bad. I wasn't, he told them, nearly as ferocious or as unreasonable as people thought.

I suppose it's that kind of result, tepid as it may be, that I'm hoping for from readers of this book.

This collection of articles is taken from eight years of a proudly—some might say defiantly—feminist column that appeared every Saturday in the St. John's *Evening Telegram*.

It was after one of those angry exchanges of opinion that give us feminists such a bad name that I strangely and unexpectedly fell into the role of weekly columnist. City Editor Sean Finlay was seething at the news that the December, 1984, issue of *Penthouse* had been stopped and recalled by Justice departments across the country in response to concerns of the National Action Committee on the Status of Women. He was already annoyed by the campaign our Coalition of Citizens Against Pornography had been waging. In an editorial, he raked me over the coals, referring to me by name no less than twelve times.

I was allowed space to reply, and we continued to spar on the editorial pages of the paper, not only on pornography but on issues referring to women's place in society generally.

After two years of this there came a thaw and an invitation to lunch. Would I like to write a weekly column for the paper? Sean asked. "Can it be an unabashedly feminist column, with my own personal biases—political and otherwise—and will it appear in such a manner that it is addressed to both men and women?" He said "of course" to each of my queries and added, "We would hardly be offering you the job if we were going to tell you what you could write. I like your style and occasionally you make some good points." He was as good as his word and from that moment on I had support and generosity from him and the other editors whom I gradually came to know.

It turned out to be one of those experiences that renews my faith and optimism. The editors and I approached things from very different backgrounds. We could have been enemies in the normal course of events but, as time went by, I think we learned a lot from each other and became friends in the process.

After I'd been at the paper for quite some time, one of the editors suggested that when I started I must have thought they were a bunch of male chauvinists. "No," I lied, "but I thought you hadn't examined the facts." He allowed as how that was true. Strangely and sadly, the only interference I ever encountered was when a woman took over the editor's job and, at her first opportunity, used a hatchet on words that were important to me.

My first column appeared on December 6, 1986. Since that time I've heard from people in all walks of life: men and women, young and old, rich and poor. People have stopped me in supermarkets, bank line-ups, at restaurants and theatres and on the streets of communities from Labrador to the south coast of Newfoundland. Nearly all begin by saying, "I don't always agree with you, but..." What comes after that is acknowledgement of some point or points I had made in a column. We often go on to argue analyses or conclusions, but the important thing is that we have found common ground and can have a constructive discussion.

If people want to argue, that's fine with me. I wanted the columns to encourage public introspection and to provoke helpful debate. They were intended to put the spotlight on what we've been doing that has caused women to be treated as inferior beings, with all the destructive fallout that implies for members of both sexes.

Feminism is a struggle for equality and for women's right to be heard. This collection is intended to keep the debate going. The way I see it, as long as we're talking to each other we've got a chance to sort things out.

When I became pregnant with my first child, I stopped running and began walking cautiously, protectively. Taking care became instinctive until the nine months were up and my baby was safely delivered.

When he was a year old, his father and I joined the British Columbia anti-radiation-hazards committees to ban bomb-testing. It was the least we could do to protect our child, and others, from the effects of radioactive strontium-90 falling from the skies.

Two years later I searched until I found a doctor who would allow me to have my second newborn son in the room with me. It was called "rooming in" and was a first for the General Hospital in Vancouver.

Two years after that, our adopted daughter came to us and ever since our lives have been wondrously shaped by all three of them. When we fight for causes, it's their world we care about.

If it's your cup of tea, parenthood is wonderful. It suited us down to the ground and I have cherished every moment of it. Somewhere along the way my husband and I happily agreed that I should be a stay-at-home mother. We both wanted children with full-time parents and realized how lucky we were to have this choice.

But there was a small unidentifiable ache that grew during those early years of motherhood. At first, I was barely conscious of it. It was only when I read Betty Friedan's *The Feminine Mystique* that I recognized with astonishment that my ache was one shared by thousands of women. As mothers and wives, we yearned for something more. And felt terrible guilt at not being satisfied with having so much.

The opening chapter of Friedan's book is entitled "The Problem That Has No Name," referring to the voice within women that said, "No matter how cherished, I want something more than my husband and my children and my home." It was a revelation; for the first time I felt the load lightened because I didn't have to feel guilty anymore. I was normal. My longing to get back into the field of social work, which I loved, wasn't an aberration. Freidan said it was okay to want to feel like a separate person as well as an appendage.

Young women and men today won't know what I'm talking about but women over fifty can remember. So many doors were closed. Women were second-class citizens in almost every regard. But in the years that this phase of the women's movement was gestating, *The Feminine Mystique* was a rivetting catalyst. The ferment led to the establishment of the Royal Commission on the Status of Women, and their comprehensive report began the unravelling of the sordid story of women's inequality across the country.

Every social event we went to in the sixties had people talking about The Book. When I was asked if I had read it, my husband would cut in with, "Read it? She's written it!" But he was teasing while listening and thinking and arguing with me over Friedan's conclusions.

A friend of ours had a tougher ride. Every time she lost the Friedan argument with her rigid husband she went out and bought a new hat. She had a cupboard full of divine hats before she finally sued for divorce. But it was a classic case of a marriage that could have been saved had he ever been able to break from his traditional upbringing. His mother had done everything for him except chew his food. He thought his wife should do the same, for him and for their three children.

We once spent a weekend with them at a summer resort. We emptied our car of the three children, the suitcases, the pram, the beach apparatus, the food. One of us changed diapers while the other started supper.

At the cabin next door Jack had picked up his golf clubs from the trunk of their car and waved that he would see us at supper. He strolled out to the greens and left his wife to cope with the unpacking and the three babies. I knew she had been crying when one of us went over to give her a hand.

In today's world it seems impossible to comprehend that a man could be so insensitive and so brutally selfish. But Jack's behaviour was not untypical of the traditional male, and it serves as a reminder of why there had to be a women's movement in Canada.

At every turn men like him were reinforced by laws and customs that told them they were right. Women were lesser creatures. Both church and state sent out messages that women were born to serve quietly without expectation of reward, at least on this earth.

Feminists set out to change all that.

1 The Way We Were

My answers may disturb the experts and women alike, for they imply social change. But...I believe that women can affect society, as well as be affected by it; that, in the end, a woman, as a man, has the power to choose, and to make her own heaven or hell.

The Feminine Mystique, Betty Friedan, 1962.

BUT WHAT ABOUT WOMEN?

In 1857, women garment workers marched through the streets of New York, protesting dreadful working conditions, child labour, 12-hour working days, and minuscule pay. They were beaten by police. In 1908 the same union of women marched again for similar demands, but added the call for equal pay and for the vote for women. Their slogan was "Bread and Roses;" bread to symbolize economic security and roses to symbolize the beauty in life. Inspired by their banners, James Oppenheim wrote the poem that in later years was set to music by Mimi Farina, sister to Joan Baez.

The anniversary of the demonstration, March 8, has become a day of celebration for women all over the world and is known as "International Women's Day." The song has become an anthem to many of us in the feminist movement and is as stirring as "We Shall Overcome" was to the civil rights movement. Here are the words:

> As we go marching, marching,
> In the beauty of the day,
> A million darkened kitchens,
> A thousand mill lofts grey
> Are touched with all the radiance
> That a sudden sun discloses.
> For the people hear us singing,
> Bread and Roses, Bread and Roses.

> As we go marching, marching,
> We battle too for men,
> For they are women's children
> And we'll mother them again.
> Our lives shall not be sweated
> From birth until life closes
> Hearts starve as well as bodies
> Give us bread, but give us roses.
>
> As we go marching, marching,
> Unnumbered women dead
> Go crying through our singing
> Their ancient call for bread.
> Small art and love and beauty
> Their drudging spirits knew.
> Yes, it is bread we fight for,
> But we fight for roses too.
>
> As we go marching, marching,
> We bring the greater days.
> The rising of the women
> Is the rising of the race.
> No more the drudge and idler,
> Ten that toil where one reposes.
> But a sharing of life's glories:
> Bread and Roses, Bread and Roses.

Years ago, when labour organizations were becoming more visible, speakers at public rallies were often taunted with the cry, "But what about the workers?" The phrase, repeated many times, later became something of a joke. Today there is another cry and politicians have learned it is no joke. Women working for equality have become a force to be reckoned with, and now when party leaders and policy makers make pronouncements, they must be prepared to answer the question, "But what about women?"

In the 1984 federal election, the three party leaders engaged in two nationally televised debates: one on general election issues, and one—the first of its kind—devoted entirely to issues determined by women. The 1986 first ministers' conference promised that "women's issues" would be high on the agenda. Every provincial government had to put in place a minister responsible for the status of women and a special advisory council on the status of women. The federal government had to do this too.

None of this recognition happened by itself; nor did it happen overnight. It is the result of a continuing struggle by women the world over, a struggle that has gone on for centuries. It has cost enormous sacrifice and a lot of plain, hard work.

Women have chained themselves to the pillars of the British House of Commons, fought lengthy court battles, worked within political parties and outside of them, organized marches and filled their lives with meetings. Women have earned every ounce of recognition they now enjoy, and they have accomplished a lot.

We now have the vote. Women are now—since 1929—legally defined as "persons." The 1982 Charter passed with the Constitution Act has a guarantee that the rights and freedoms it defines apply equally to women and men. The provincial Matrimonial Property Act ensures that assets will be divided equally between wife and husband. More women are getting into professional schools. Women are now seen on television as news broadcasters. Major universities have programs of women's studies. Labour federations are electing more women to senior positions. Banks now grant mortgages to women. Girls can take industrial arts, boys can learn to cook. As the cigarette ad said, "We've come a long way, baby!"

But all is not yet sweetness and light. It is true that our arguments are finally getting through to some people. Something called "the women's vote" is beginning to haunt our more alert politicians, but the opposition has not died away. Sometimes we get results and sometimes we get something pretending to be results. Too often we get the old smoke and mirror trick; it looks good until the smoke clears and we see what happened.

The 1986 federal-provincial conference is a case in point. Ballyhooed in advance by the Prime Minister of Canada as the time when women's concerns would be high on the agenda and were foremost in his heart, what happened? Well, nothing much. "Economic equality for women," which was supposed to be a central issue, stayed on the back burner. Our own premier went to the conference without an adviser on women's issues and presented a paper giving lip-service to ideals of equality, full of self-congratulations and totally devoid of any new initiatives.

After days of pronouncements from the prime minister that it was his earnest desire to appoint women to empty senate seats, what happened? A woman was appointed all right, but more on the grounds of her husband's identity than on deserving the position in her own right.

Yes, we have come a long way, but we still have a long way to go.

The changes that women have fought for, and the ones we fight for now, affect every aspect of society—our language, our workplaces, our family responsibilities. When women's lives change, so do men's. Some changes are hard for some people to accept, and some can create new problems. But the struggle goes on, fuelled by hope that the changes will come.

SYSTEMIC DISCRIMINATION

I don't think there is a facet of our lives that hasn't been affected by the women's movement, all over the world. In 1972, my husband and I visited the United Nations Assembly and were taken through the building by a pleasant, intelligent young tour guide I have never forgotten. As we moved from room to room, she explained the work of the organization, its many complex responsibilities. Finally, she sat us down in a lecture hall where we were shown slides as she continued her explanations.

To my astonishment, in the middle of her talk, she referred to the women's liberation movement and the stirrings in various countries where feminist issues were beginning to surface. When she spoke of "women's libbers" (as we were called then), there was a predictable response: a little ripple of amusement as though the audience was anticipating something funny.

It was understandable. The image of the women's movement presented by the media in those days was usually the most sensational or the silliest. Like any social movement we had—and still have—our share of crackpots and people who tried the wrong tactic at the wrong time, and it was on those that the journalists usually concentrated. They played women's movement stories for laughs and rarely bothered to examine the serious issues.

Sitting in front of us in the UN lecture hall was an American father with his teenage daughter and son. All three scoffed and snickered when the guide mentioned women's lib. It caught the attention of the guide and she concentrated on them as she went on with her talk.

The attitude of the men, she said, was not unusual or surprising: it is difficult for men to see that they have advantages that are not available to women. Then she focused on the young girl in the now rather uncomfortable American family and said something like, "My dear, the men may laugh because they don't understand, but you shouldn't laugh. It is imperative that you begin to understand the role of women in American society."

In her own South Asian country, she told us, it was extremely rare for women to get education, or to be able to do anything with their lives beyond bearing babies and cooking meals. Women in the western world, she said, could aspire to wider experiences but they were still far from being on an equal footing with men. Those who worked outside the home earned a bit more than half of men's salaries; women were not represented in any significant number in medicine, law, universities, as heads of unions or business, or as elected representatives and policy makers.

The facts and figures that the tour guide was giving us were drawn from research and analysis that the women's movement was just beginning to undertake at the time and has gone on to broaden and deepen ever since. It added up to a picture of the situation that we have come to refer to as "systemic discrimination." That young tour guide did a good job of describing its effects, but it is one of the most difficult ideas to get across to people who are not familiar with the arguments.

It is easy enough for reasonable people today to see that denying women the vote was intolerable. Equally unthinkable in our enlightened age is the notion that women should be denied the right to be defined in law as "persons," or that they should be given fewer rights than men under the Canadian Charter of Rights and Freedoms.

Yet in all three of these cases, intelligent, rational, reasonable people, both men and women, were convinced that the denial of rights to women was completely proper and sensible. Three successive Canadian prime ministers and five judges of the Supreme Court could see no reason why women should be legally defined as persons. In 1981, almost the entire machinery of provincial and federal governments could see no reason to entrench women's rights in the Canadian Charter. In each case, women had to protest and argue and struggle for years to bring about the changes that we now so easily take for granted.

It is the sort of experience that has helped the women's movement to understand the significance of systemic discrimination. Denying women the vote or a place in the Charter of Rights is only the end product of a process of socialization that begins at birth. Girl babies and boy babies are treated differently almost from the beginning. If a girl baby happens to be put into something blue it is of no great concern but boys must never, ever be found in pink. Soon the little boys are being told that big boys don't cry; crying is for girls and sissies. As they grow older, boys are given hockey sticks, trucks, and tools while their sisters get dolls and make-up kits.

Boys are encouraged to be doers, and girls learn their "proper" role as spectators. When they are grown up, the young man will expect his dinner date to sit enraptured as he tells of his accomplishments. She will have been instructed by countless magazine articles in how to be a good listener and how to shore up a male ego. If they should attend meetings together, the male voice is likely to be the dominant one—it's only "natural," after all.

An understanding of systemic discrimination leads to another important insight. Since our socialization process has defined men as "naturally" superior, it is men who have filled the positions of power. Therefore, when women have struggled and protested, they have mostly had to do it against men. But what looks like a battle of the sexes is not really that at all. It is not a matter of women fighting against men, it is people who have been the victims of discrimination fighting to change the system that discriminates against them.

Unfortunately, it is often hard for both men and women to realize this. When women attack the entrenched power of men, it is hard for the men who hold it not to feel threatened. And because men hold the power, it is hard for women not to see men, rather than the system, as the enemy. In fact, most men are victims of the system, too, and suffer from unemployment and insufficient wages and arbitrary decisions by power-brokers.

What needs to be understood by all parties is that the feminist movement is not an attack against men. It is an attack against a system of discrimination. The battles we have won so far have been won because we have been able to convince people of both sexes that the system was wrong.

Of course, we haven't convinced everybody. Some men will continue to defend their positions of privilege and to demean and abuse women. They are products of the system and they will continue to be targets in the battle to change it. The encouraging thing is that more and more they are coming to be the targets not just for women, but also for men who see the inequities we have been struggling against and are joining in the struggle.

In the meantime, St. John's in the late 1980s saw an interesting example of systemic discrimination at work. It was announced that three high schools under the Roman Catholic School Board were to become co-educational collegiates. The two that were all-boys schools were to keep their names, but the one that was an all-girls school would have to have a new name. Apparently it is all right for girls to attend an erstwhile boys' school, but it doesn't work the other way around. Our educational systems teach a lot more than what is in the curriculum. The lesson in this case seems clear.

I am happy to report that, after a good deal of objection and protest, Holy Heart of Mary High School retained its historic name. So far as is known, none of the male students now attending has suffered unduly.

A WOMEN'S LIBBER? NO WAY!

One year when a federal government task force was visiting St. John's, I attended a social function to meet the commissioners and their staff. It was the usual kind of party with easy, superficial talk that occasionally turned to more serious discussion. It also had, as I remember, some great Newfoundland music and superb fish dishes which everyone seemed to enjoy. Out of all the lighthearted chatter, there is one conversation that lingers in my mind.

It was with a small group that included a young woman who held a very senior position as assistant to a cabinet minister who travelled the world. Her role was almost equal to his in negotiating trade agreements with various countries. She amused the four of us in her conversation circle by describing the lack of understanding she frequently encountered. Her minister would often find it necessary to inform the host delegation in some African or Asian country that this woman was not there to hang up coats or pour coffee, but would actually sit down at the bargaining table with them. Not only that, but she would take an active part in the negotiations. In many places, their hosts were amazed to see a woman performing such a role, she said.

I found her stories interesting and amusing until I heard her say, "Of course I believe in equal pay. But I'm no women's libber." My reaction, of course, was predictable. But before I had time to respond I was surprised and pleased to hear her three male colleagues pounce: "What do you mean by dumping on the women's movement? You wouldn't be doing half of what you're doing now if they hadn't opened doors for you."

The three men had understood the messages of the women's movement and were supportive of equality rights, while the woman who had benefitted so much from the work of other women was disclaiming any connection.

The irony didn't stop there, either. I learned that this ministerial assistant who was not a "women's libber" had a young son who attended an excellent daycare centre in Ottawa. The boy was lovingly cared for by his father who took full charge while the mother was travelling.

Not too long ago it was common to hear fathers bragging about never having changed a diaper or heated a bottle. Today many young fathers take pride in being nurturers and cementing bonds with their infant children. In a remarkably short time, a lot of things have changed. This rising young civil servant had many advantages that her predecessors lacked: a changed social climate, quality daycare and an affirmative action program (whether voluntary or mandatory) that has worked within the government service.

It is perhaps understandable that women who work hard and do well in their careers can sometimes fail to recognize how many thousands of women helped to make it happen. But it has also been said that if we don't learn from our history we live to repeat it. Women would do well to take that message to heart.

No woman can possibly know all the wheels that have been turned to open the door for her advancement. What she can know, however, is that it is only very recently that women have been able to entertain any reasonable expectation of reaching the top. When those women of today who have made it insist that they have done it all on their own, are they suggesting that all the women before them were incompetent?

This brings me to a news story in *The Evening Telegram* about six women who gained senior positions in the provincial government. Their opinions on how they got there are varied. Some recognized that there had been changes in social attitudes, but seemed to treat the changes as though they were the product of natural forces and had nothing to do with anybody's deliberate intention. Others acknowledged the women's movement and the pressure for affirmative action.

One of the six rather grudgingly admitted that "it is possible some opportunities open to women today wouldn't exist if it were not for the pushier part of the women's movement." However, like the federal ministerial assistant I started with, she does not want to be identified with feminists.

"What do you mean by feminist?" she asked the reporter, "I'm not a bra-burner, and I don't go out on the streets arguing and shouting." Hard-nosed feminists, she believes, turn people off.

I despair when I hear anybody using the silly, meaningless term "bra-burner" as a put-down. The plain fact is that without a lot of arguing and shouting and hard-nosed pushing, women wouldn't even be able to vote, let alone hold good government jobs. More recently, it took a good deal of arguing and shouting and, yes, demonstrating in the streets before women's rights were included in the Charter of Rights and Freedoms. And every woman in Canada benefitted from the work that went into that endeavour. But that's the way social revolutions happen.

Of course, the people in the front lines are open to attack, ridicule, and scorn. In 1973, when a front-line St. John's feminist appeared on a radio phone-in show, the host started things off by asking her whether or not she was wearing a brassiere. He could get away with it then, but if he tried it today he'd be clobbered. That woman's hard-nosed efforts led the way to improvements for all women, and are partly responsible for the present social climate that allows women greater opportunities than ever before.

Women who have made it have of course worked hard to get where they are, and some are terrified that anybody might use the familiar put-down that their success is "just because they are women." Besides, when top management promote, they are much more prone to choose someone who doesn't identify herself as a feminist. And some just don't know the history; they take the present situation for granted and don't inquire as to how it got that way. A few try to have the best of both worlds—they will use the demands and accomplishments of the women's movement to further their own careers, but carefully avoid any identification with the group.

Whatever the reasons, though, I always find it a little bit sad when women find it necessary to distance themselves from the social movement that has done so much to improve their status in our society. Feminists see their responsibility as opening doors for all women. As Rosemary Brown puts it, "Until all of us has made it, none of us has made it."

THE ROYAL COMMISSION AND THE FEMINIZATION OF POWER

During the 1960s, pressure on the federal government by women's groups grew steadily, until it was impossible for the politicians to ignore any longer the cry for attention to the inequalities faced by women in Canadian society. A Royal Commission on the Status of Women was announced, with Florence Bird (now Senator) as chairperson.

The report, released in 1970, affirmed the many claims of injustice that women's organizations had been making. It produced statistical evidence that women were suffering discrimination at every turn: in employment, wages, opportunities, training, child responsibilities and legal rights. Strong recommendations were presented to government for action.

Women's groups, responsible for the establishment of the Commission, were well aware of the time-honoured Canadian strategy of setting up parliamentary commissions to get governments off the hook. The practice was all too familiar: public hearings held, report submitted, recommendations presented—all with maximum publicity—so that the general public ends up assuming that government has done something. The women knew better: they knew the report would join all the other ones on dusty House of Commons shelves and nothing would come of the recommendations unless they made it happen.

Preliminary meetings were held that led to the formation of the National Action Committee on the Status of Women, with delegates from various women's groups. They were some of the strangest meetings I have ever attended. It was still a time when upper-middle-class women felt it important to wear white gloves and fancy hats, but it was also a time when young people were experimenting with a whole range of styles.

It was not unusual to see a cluster of women involved in intense discussion, some wearing mink and silk, and others bib overalls and work-boots. Working-class women, professionals, business women, artists and housewives listened and contributed as they compared notes about injustices taking place in the workplace and in the home.

These were women who normally would never be in the same room together. I used to leave these meetings in wonderment, believing that if we could cross so many barriers and stay friends, then we could accomplish almost anything together.

"They're not just talking *at* each other," I would say to my neighbour. "They are honestly listening to one another. They want to hear the other's viewpoint."

There was a lot to talk about. We were just starting to examine the many discriminatory practices affecting women in every phase of life. More research was undertaken. More briefs were composed. Information was shared. All the usual things were done that are necessary in the formation of a new organization. What we didn't realize at the time was that we were also doing something else of great importance. We were working out our own ways of getting things done.

A new style of democracy was emerging, one that relied more on reaching consensus than it did on arbitrary methods of majority voting.

The head table went. Who needs a head table to separate "important" people from the rank and file? We looked for round tables to get away from the old-fashioned, male, authoritarian model where the chair is given ultimate power and is placed at the head of the long table to remind everyone of the fact. We buried the gavel and resisted complicated rules of order. We wanted to encourage debate, not close it off—even if at times it meant tedium. We encouraged rotation so that more women could contribute, gain experience, develop confidence. We weren't looking for "stars;" we were looking for ways in which more women could feel *empowered*. In feminism, that's the key word that describes the heart of the matter. We tried to share not only burdens, but rewards and experience. We scorned back-room decision-making and made it easy for our representatives to be accountable to us.

This "feminization of power," as it has been called, is much closer to true democracy than you can get with Roberts' Rules of Order. It may, in fact, be more threatening to the boys in authority than any of our specific demands.

Our society has been based on a system of patriarchy, where we have been taught that men are valuable and women are not. We are determined to change that system, but the process by which we bring about change is as important to feminists as is the final goal.

Penny Kome, author of *Play From Strength*, a publication of the Canadian Advisory Council on the Status of Women (1983), put it this way:

Men's organizations have evolved along the lines of the military and the corporation: hierarchical, with one boss at the top of a clear chain of command. Women's organizations have evolved, to a great extent, from family roles and from egalitarian groups like volunteer societies, church and professional clubs. The result is that women tend to be "team players" who make sure the work gets done and don't care who gets the credit. Women are also more likely than men to worry about hurting someone else's feelings. This concern for the process as well as the goal can be a handicap for women when working in a group with men—or it can be women's greatest organizing strength when working with other women.

2 Women's Place

How does a society determine its mores? Larger messages are often so subtle and intricately woven into everything we do that we don't realize the effect.

> Patriarchy is a social system which supports and authenticates the predominance of men, brings about a concentration of power and privilege in the hands of men and, consequently, leads to the control and subordination of women, generating social inequality between the sexes.
>
> This disparity of power, privilege and prestige entrenches and perpetuates patriarchy in society. It gives men power, domination and advantage over women and explains much of the continuing violence.
> "Heritage of Violence," Social Affairs Committee of the Assembly of Quebec Bishops, 1989

WEREN'T THERE ANY WOMEN?

A while ago, I found myself fantasizing about being a teacher and giving my students a special lesson in history and civics.

It was still in my mind later, when I was waiting for a friend in the lobby of Confederation Building, Newfoundland's legislature, and I started to wonder what it would be like for a teacher bringing her or his class to see their provincial government in action.

As the bus drove up, they'd pass the statue of Gaspar Corte-Real, looking like one of those super-heroes from the Saturday morning cartoons. Gaspar looks as though he has just spotted the villain over by the College of Fisheries. In front of the Confederation Building steps, they'd pass John Cabot gazing thoughtfully out to sea through the Narrows. Down to the left, they'd see Wilfred Grenfell looking every inch the Labrador doctor, ready for any emergency with his parka and medical bag.

Inside, they'd pass through the lobby with its rows of bronze busts of former prime ministers, nineteen of them, from Philip F. Little (1855-1858) to Frederick C. Alderdice (1928; 1932-1934).

Once upstairs, they'd be ushered into the visitors' gallery in the House of Assembly. Now, before they've heard a word spoken in the House, what have they learned?

They may not realize it consciously, but having passed an array of figures from their history, and gazing down on the contemporary decision-makers of their province, they have received a powerful message. Among the contemporary decision-makers, they would have seen few women; few are elected, still fewer appointed to Cabinet. At times, among the symbols of what is important and memorable in their society, they may have seen one woman, or none at all.

The atmosphere in the House, even on a good day, would be that of a men's club—maybe even a locker room. If things were running true to form, the teacher might begin to get nervous. The antics of the MHAs might begin to remind the visitors of a classroom full of junior high school boys with a substitute teacher, and the decision might be made to leave a bit early and take the pupils back down to the lobby to look around a bit before heading back to school.

They didn't take time to look at it on the way up, but one of the dominant features of the lobby is a big mural over the archway, depicting 500 years of their history. Prepared sheets from the information desk would help the students identify its many fascinating elements.

John Cabot is there, of course, and Sir Humphrey Gilbert, and a Viking, and a Beothuk Indian man in feathers and paint. There are veterans of the three armed services, and a mountie. A father and two sons are hauling up a boat, four men and a boy are laying out a fish net, and three men are logging. MacKenzie King is there, and Louis St. Laurent, and Joseph R. Smallwood. There's a Newfoundland dog, and a horse and cart, and a paper mill. It's a very nice painting.

But, do you know, unless you count Captain Bob Bartlett's schooner, the Effie M. Morrissey, there is not one woman to be seen?

There *is* a little girl sitting on a rock. And that small figure with its back to us: that could be another little girl—I'm not sure. And away off to the left, far in the distance, there's a priest in front of a small flock of parishioners: the little gathering is too small to be seen very clearly, but there's almost certainly a woman or two among them. There would have to be, in a religious grouping.

And so it goes. In another corner of the lobby is a touching remembrance of those who died in the wars, with these words: "...Every country is home to one man and exile to another. Where a man died bravely at one with his destiny, that soil is his." No one would want to take away one shred of the respect due to the memory of the men who gave up their lives, but weren't women in the armed forces too?

There *is* one woman remembered in the lobby: a plaque to Margot Davies, MBE, whose wartime broadcasts from Britain endeared her to the people of Newfoundland. Strangely, though, it gives no details of where she came from, or where she lived, or when she was born and died.

All around, I ended up pretty depressed about the message those schoolchildren would be picking up. Would the girls feel shyer and less adequate after their visit? Would the boys feel a bit stronger, more in charge and more ready to perpetuate the inequalities of the past? Maybe it isn't as direct and immediate as that, but it is a powerful message nonetheless, coming from the most official source in the land.

I'm not suggesting that this wonderful mural was painted with malice aforethought. It went up in 1960. The artist chose the symbols that he felt were important for a reflection of Newfoundland history, and his choice very clearly demonstrates the societal attitudes of the time. Most of us, including me, would not have noticed the omission of women from the picture.

But—if I were the teacher now, I would be asking the children to examine what the omission has meant to women. We might also study the report of the Royal Commission on the Status of Women which came out ten years later.

Obviously, we can't rewrite history. The nineteen prime ministers *were* all men. But if we really wanted to change the messages we give our children we would introduce them to the truth about women—in the past and in the present. Our most prestigious government building, in our capital city, could find any number of ways to honour and record the work of the remarkable women of Newfoundland.

THE PATRIARCHAL SYSTEM

One of the more difficult ideas feminists have been trying to get across is the recognition that women and men grow up in different cultures. Many find that difficult to accept because our own experiences seem "natural." We're used to the male culture being the dominant one in every sphere of our lives.

Critical decisions about society have been and continue to be made by men. We operate under male agendas, we follow male methods of organization and we respond to male priorities.

Not only is that patently unfair to 52 percent of the population, there are also a number of negative cultural activities that are purely male (though not practised by all men) that we could happily do without.

Women do not have a traditional equivalent to stag parties, nor the macho experience of locker rooms. Rape and pornography are male inventions. Young boys are taught by older men to go out on the hockey rink to practice violence. It is the male culture that has promoted war. And yet this is the culture that has shaped our leaders.

A 1988 article in the *Globe and Mail* brought home an aspect of male culture that sickeningly illustrates how some men are socialized.

The author told of his experiences at an unnamed university in the 1970s. As a first-year student he was a frequent guest at a fraternity house where a good friend of his resided. He found that he greatly enjoyed the pleasant atmosphere, good food and stimulating conversation. Although fraternities had gone out of style during the 1960s due to their elitist exclusiveness, they were trying to make a comeback and he was invited to join.

He had one reservation only. The social club he enjoyed, but he made it clear to his friend and the other members that he would rather not join if it included initiation rites which involved either physical or psychological distress. The fraternity brothers gave him their assurances that he had nothing to worry about; initiation was simply good fun that he would find quite enjoyable. He trusted them and applied to join.

He described the horror that followed. He was, first of all, confined to a closet for twelve hours where he became quite disoriented. Then he was led out of the closet blindfolded and taken to a room where he was forced to kneel with his chin on a table. When the blindfold was removed he was facing a barrage of high wattage lamps.

From behind the lights voices yelled abuse at him and shouted obscenities about his family. They spat out humiliating questions and demanded that he reply. "The insults and questions succeeded each other at a dizzying rate," he wrote. "I felt quite ill. So much so, in fact, that I decided to leave, wondering vaguely whether I should call the police."

When his so-called friends realized he wanted to leave, they stopped the questioning, repeating that it was all a joke and returned him to the closet.

He described how later he asked house members why they had lied to him and done these terrible things. Their defence was that "they had been sworn to secrecy at the time of their own initiations...it had all been an innocent exercise in bonding...it was all in good fun." And the familiar phrase—"it had made men out of them."

One almost incredible fact is that the unseen interrogators were not only the young men of the fraternity. Some of them were men who had graduated years before and were now respected professionals. "I cannot help but wonder about the motivation of those involved," the writer said. "What could a doctor, lawyer, or judge possibly be doing behind those lights, happily engaged in breaking down young men to the best of their ability?"

What is so awful is that these men enjoyed their friend's agony—or those who didn't lacked the courage to break ranks. If a boy begins life as a decent, kind-hearted fellow, what does it do to him to join this sort of secret society? I would guess that it makes him very tolerant of other people's suffering.

Most of us have thought and hoped that the brutality of repressive political regimes like the ones that happened in Chile and El Salvador could never happen here. But stories like this one aren't reassuring. The patriarchal system relies on secrecy and complicity and makes it unpleasant for those who resist. Many men won't thank the author for writing this article but the rest of us will.

In 1995, we were all shocked by videotapes of revolting initiation rituals in the Canadian military, said to have been witnessed by senior officers. "Men will be boys," we used to say. And boys will one day be men.

SPORTING WOMEN

One of the last places I would have expected to find a feminist tract would be among the publications of the federal government's department of Fitness and Amateur Sport. But I have read a remarkable document that was released in October of 1986 by that very department, and I'm impressed.

The purpose of the booklet is to present specific policies and plans to improve the role of women in sports. Such action is needed, the authors say, because;

> Unfortunately, history has demonstrated that opportunities for women to develop as either participants or leaders at any level in the sport system have been significantly fewer than those made available to men.

The booklet reviews events and initiatives that have led up to an inequitable situation. In the process, intentionally or not, it presents a capsule history of the women's movement in Canada.

Sport Canada held its first national conference on women and sport in 1974. This historic event was motivated in part by recommendations made in 1970 by the Royal Commission on the Status of Women, which had noted, among many other things, the unequal participation of girls and boys in sports at Canadian schools. Another motivation for the conference was that the following year, 1975, had been declared International Women's Year by the United Nations. It *is* gratifying to note that our own province was one of the first to pick up on the challenge; in 1975, it co-sponsored the Newfoundland and Labrador Conference on Women and Sport.

Further conferences and actions followed, leading to such things as the formation in 1981 of the Canadian Association for the Advancement of Women in Sport, a national organization that has as its objective to "promote, develop and advocate a feminist perspective on women and sport."

Not surprisingly, women working on issues in the field of sports turned up with the same sort of analyses and findings as women working in business, education, health care, and so on. The booklet informs us, for example, that in sports, as in the other fields, "women were playing a major role in carrying out the work, but were seriously under-represented in the decision-making process."

What I find both remarkable and impressive is the way the booklet summarizes and explains the issues.

Consider the following:

> Like the majority of Canadian institutions, sport is essentially dominated by men. Although Canadian society is less patriarchal than in years gone by, some structural injustices are so deeply rooted in the general arrangements of society that they escape notice.
>
> For example, a ten-year old girl who wishes to play organized competitive sport may be as talented, as fit and, in some cases, stronger and faster than her male counterpart. And yet, because of the traditional rules or mandate of the sport organization in question, she is unable to participate because of her gender. Another example can be found in the disproportionate number of events on the Olympic Calendar for men and women. These kinds of structural injustices—generally in the form of a complete lack of or very limited opportunity for female sport involvement—do not discriminate against any single individual female, but discriminate against females as a group.

With a few changes of wording that could apply to almost any field of endeavour. So could this:

> The majority of females have, for a long period of time, been subjected to informal types of discrimination. Traditionally, young girls are not necessarily discouraged from being physically active but are not given the same kinds of encouragement that boys receive. Over a period of time, this subtle form of discrimination has long-term detrimental effects on the quality and quantity of female participation in sport. The traditional roles ascribed to girls and women have severely restricted their participation rates. If young people do not see women in roles related to sport and physical activity, a process of restrictive and adverse sex-stereotyping begins to take shape. Unless this situation is changed, the advancement of women in sport will be severely hampered.

This is what Sport Canada set out as its overall goal with respect to women's participation:

> Equality implies that women at all levels of the sport system should have an equal opportunity to participate. Equality is not

necessarily meant to imply that women wish to participate in the same activities as men, but rather to indicate that activities of their choice should be provided and administered in a fair and unbiased environment.

At all levels of the sport system, equal opportunities must exist for women and men to compete, coach, officiate or administer sport.

The purpose of this goal is to create an environment in which no one is forced into a pre-determined role or status because of gender.

It would be interesting to know how many of our school boards and athletic institutions have adopted the Sport Canada policies.

KILLING ME SOFTLY

In 1980 the National Film Board of Canada released a Jean Kilbourne film entitled *Killing Me Softly*. Those were early days in the awakening of women across the country. A lot of opportunities for women that we now take for granted did not exist. We were just starting to document the sexism that was rampant in society. Some women were worried about the pornography industry that was just making news; most women didn't have the faintest idea what the fuss was all about.

We were trying at the time to understand the forces that shape us. We were analyzing the messages society sends out and where those messages come from. Where does sexism get reinforced? And by whom? There were, and are, many contenders. School text books are one. The schools themselves are another. Movies and magazines, sports and professions all help. But it didn't take long for studies to point a finger at a major contributor—the advertising industry.

Advertising has incredible power to enhance or distort images of human beings. In magazines, on television, on billboards, in window displays, in offices, banks and department stores, advertisers compete for our attention. We absorb their messages as we buy our newspaper and when our children watch cartoons. We are bombarded with hundreds and thousands of images that we add to our mental computer banks. And these images condition us. Television is one of the most powerful educational forces in society. It helps form our attitudes about people and, consequently, it can shape our behaviour.

Women were beginning to be aware of this. We had objected to the industry's suggestion that women were another kind of consumer product. Letters and briefs were written to manufacturers objecting to their practice of using women as sexual objects to sell cars, trips abroad, brands of liquor. I had been part of these deliberations, so I felt fairly knowledgeable about the subject when I went along to see the film mentioned earlier. But I wasn't at all prepared for what I saw.

In scene after scene, women were used in degrading and violent poses. There were children dressed and posed in sexually provocative ways. Both women and children were presented as collections of body parts, without humanity.

The women watching the film were sick and silent as it ended. What we had been watching was not pornography, but a simple collection of familiar advertisements that we were all seeing all the time, every day. Separately they didn't look all that harmful. We might have thought them distasteful or stupid, but no more. When they were all put together, though, we got the full impact of what the industry was saying about women and children. And it wasn't nice at all.

After the showing we talked to each other about what we had seen, about what could be done to change these destructive images, about recognizing the influence these ads have in homes where a woman is already being battered or where a child is being abused. We were beginning to realize that advertising was not only denying us positions of respect and equal status but, in fact, was contributing to the forces of violence against women and children

The film made a powerful and lasting impact. I've never forgotten the role that negative images play in reinforcing the victimization of women and children. But you really need to see the barrage of messages brought together before you can understand what it is that they are saying collectively.

In isolation, they don't look all that important.

The pornography and advertising industries have continued to grow in scope and complexity. And as the problem did not go away, neither did Jean Kilbourne. In 1989, she produced another film on the subject. The title? *Still Killing Me Softly*.

AGNES MACPHAIL WAS THE FIRST

It's never easy being the first. Agnes Macphail, as the first woman ever to sit in the House of Commons (1921), worked under enormous strain to pave the way for other women who would follow her in parliament. She used to say that as she walked down the long corridors she could almost hear their footsteps. Others along the way have carved out new traditions; the first woman Cabinet Minister, Ellen Fairclough, couldn't have found it a simple matter to push her ideas past an otherwise all-male Conservative caucus in 1957. Cairine Wilson had every eye on her as the first woman senator (1930).

Grace MacInnis was the lone woman member in the House of Commons in the late sixties. In every session of the House, she brought up the need for family planning and legalized abortions in spite of her male NDP colleagues wishing she wouldn't—and amid the hostile reactions of a totally male House.

Judy LaMarsh had her own discriminatory tales to tell of being "a woman in a gilded cage" while Liberal Cabinet Minister. Iona Campagnola has kept audiences spellbound with her stories of the glass ceiling she encountered as the first woman president of the Liberal party. She could see where decisions were being made but, even as president, was excluded from the process.

It's history now that Audrey McLaughlin of the New Democratic Party became the first woman leader of a political party in Canada in December, 1989.

"Would people vote for a party with a woman leader?" was always the question raised. Some people (well, particularly male people inside of political parties) still view women as liabilities. Nice and all that, but not someone you'd really want to trust to make important decisions.

When Agnes Macphail first ran for office, a man in her Ontario district said, "What? A woman running for Parliament? Are there no men left in Southeast Grey?" She was elected nonetheless and turned out to be one of the most sought-after orators in North America, noted for her sharp wit and forthright views. She called the House of Commons, "The House of Temptation" and the Senate, "The House of Refuge." Once, a male heckler called out from the back of a hall, "Don't you wish you were a man, Agnes Macphail?" She shot back: "Yes. Often. Don't you?"

She was a passionate defender of the common person and the rights of farmers, children, prisoners, miners and women. Here she is on farm women:

> It is true that the farmers work hard; it is true their days are long and their pay is poor. But it is also infinitely true that the farm women's day is longer and her pay poorer. With all due deference to the superior wisdom of men, one mistake that I think the men continually make in this House is that of treating the problem of rural depopulation as a man's problem and a man's problem only.
> Honourable members talk about the boy getting an education, as if when you have talked about the man and the boy you have finished the family—but you have not...The girls leave the farms first and that is pretty sure indication that the boys will leave later.

Speaking in the House of Commons, she said,

> I believe it is the desire...of everyone in this House that the home should be preserved. (But) if the preservation of the home means the enslavement of women, then we had better break it...When we have a single standard for men and women, both morally and economically, we shall have a home worth preserving.

When Agnes Macphail died, the Elizabeth Fry Society, which she had founded in Canada, took up a collection for a memorial fund to aid students of social service interested in the rehabilitation of women prisoners. And the male prisoners of Kingston penitentiary paid her a rare tribute, writing:

> Imprisonment at its best is distasteful and degrading, yet conditions today in Canadian penitentiaries are far better than they were in the 1930s when Agnes Macphail set foot within the old North Gate. The changes wrought within these cold grey walls were her handiwork: to her must go our tribute.

Occasionally I fantasize about what it would have meant to Canadian politics to have had a dozen, or fifty or a hundred Agnes Macphails in the House of Commons, year after year. The possibilities are awesome. But the reality is that it was 1935 before a second woman was elected. Martha Louise Black, aged 70, won a seat in the Yukon to replace her husband who was ill.

Three quarters of a century after Macphail, women constitute 18 percent of the members of the House of Commons.

3 Charge of the Right Brigade

> Canadians have been too complacent. We have taken democracy for granted and have not accepted personal responsibility for its survival. ...we have surrendered the decisions on our political lives to self-interested elites. Our history has been one of trust in authority, and that authority has betrayed us.
> Maude Barlow and Bruce Campbell,
> *Take Back the Nation*, Key Porter Books, 1991.

SOUNDING THE ALARM

I have received a letter addressed to "Dear Fellow Free Enterpriser" that tells me there is no time to waste. It claims that if we don't act now, "one of the most dangerous pieces of legislation ever proposed in Ontario may become law." I'm not sure what I can do about it out here in Newfoundland but I'm willing to give it a try.

This call to the barricades refers to something called Bill 154. The author of the letter, a Mr. David Somerville, says that this bill will provide for "pay police" to enter my business without a search warrant and seize my books. Does he really mean that if I lived in Toronto (God forbid) people would be bursting in and making off with my feminist collection? My Nellie McClung? My Margaret Duley?

But that's not all. Mr. Somerville says that prices will be controlled by a huge, centralized, highly authoritarian bureaucracy. Costs and prices will go up and up and up. Jobs will go down and down and down. Taxes will rise and we'll have ever more and more government. Well, at least they will in Ontario. Here in Newfoundland we've got about all we can handle already.

Mr. Somerville says he doesn't want to be an alarmist—he just wants us all to know that the economic climate of Ontario will prevent any investor from ever coming near the place again.

Well, whether he wanted to or not, he's certainly alarmed me. I haven't slept a wink for worrying about poor old Ontario going down the drain. I'd just as soon, really, that he hadn't told me about it at all. What is really alarming is that he says that all three political parties in the Ontario legislature are prepared to support this dreadful bill. Is there no end to the wickedness of Upper Canada politicians?

Astonishingly, according to Mr. Somerville, the whole thing is being proposed to deal with a problem that nobody has ever begun to prove exists. You can see why he felt compelled to write.

This infamous bill is before a standing committee, he says, who may send it to the Ontario legislature at any moment. It makes you wish they'd stop standing and sit down—or even lie down—so we could all relax a bit.

It's pretty hard to tell from Mr. Somerville's letter what this Bill 154 is all about. There was one clue, though—he's really upset because he's afraid that it "will virtually end the existence of a free labour market in Ontario." I don't think that he really meant that labour was "free" in Ontario: he probably just meant "cheap." But even if cheap labour is to be done away with, what's it all about anyway?

I was wondering about all that when I came upon another clue: "The Liberal-Socialist alliance," Mr. Somerville tells me, "says that Bill 154 is about `pay equity'." And now I start to remember. He's writing from the province that's been taking seriously the notion that women should be paid equally with men for work of equal value.

No wonder the poor man is frightened. If this keeps up, women may let it go to their heads and want to sit with legislators or with management, or stand with standing committees, or something awful like that.

Clearly, Mr. Somerville has a point to make. Nobody had a problem until now. Women knew their place and men knew theirs. Women didn't mind being paid less because they knew they were less able. Right? As he so carefully puts it, Bill 154 "means deciding how much to pay people in completely different jobs using government-imposed guidelines."

We had been getting along just fine until this nosy old busybody, do-good government of Ontario had to step in and muddle things up. You can't prove that a woman in a cleaning job works just as hard as a man collecting garbage. Who says a secretary is equal to a truck driver? Well, I mean, they can both vote, but that doesn't mean they deserve the same rate of pay, does it?

Things were bad enough when women decided that they wanted to be truck drivers too, but equal pay for work of equal value means that poor

Mr. Somerville is going to have to write endless letters and alarm all kinds of people to help him stop the mad legislators of his province.

There were all kinds of people long before him—well, I guess men mostly—who knew something like this was bound to happen if women were ever allowed to vote. The Reverend Mr. Robert Sedgewick knew what was what back in 1856, when he spoke to the Halifax YMCA. "Woman is the equal of man," he said, "in the matter of intellect, emotion and activity. But...to usurp the place of man—this was to forget her position as the complement of man—and assume a place she is incompetent to fill, or rather, was not designed to fill."

"A woman should never aspire to parliament," Mr. Sedgewick said. "Such aspirations would be resented as a presumptuous invasion of the rights of men, utterly intolerable as fairly beyond the limits of the Constitution." And he felt that factory work was not suitable either, as it would only destroy the gentle behaviour of women. Of course, in Mr. Sedgewick's day no one had gone so far as to suggest the sort of thing that Mr. Somerville has to contend with. But if he were alive today, there's no doubt whose side he'd be on.

So you see, it's not that we haven't been getting good advice along the way. Governments held back as long as they could from giving women the minimum wage, because they knew what it would lead to. In Newfoundland, women were not covered by minimum wage legislation until 1955, and even then they were quite properly paid less—fifty cents for men, thirty-five cents for women.

Some people—and I'm pretty sure Mr. Somerville and the Reverend Mr. Sedgewick would be among them—would undoubtedly date the social rot that has led to outrages like Ontario's Bill 154 to days like the fateful one in June of 1972 when Newfoundland women were given the same minimum wage as men.

I'm truly sorry if I've upset your day with all this. I don't want to be an alarmist any more than Mr. Somerville does, but we non-alarmists need your help. I wouldn't go so far as to suggest that as Ontario goes, so goes the nation. But it does make you think, doesn't it?

THEY SAID IT COULDN'T BE DONE

Some years ago Eric Kierans gave a public lecture at Memorial University on his view of Canada. He is always fascinating to listen to and, having held provincial and federal cabinet portfolios, he draws on a wealth of experience.

In one part of his talk that has stuck in my memory, he cautioned the audience not to be swayed by the clamour that comes from the big business community when any level of government is about to impose some new regulations on the way they do business. He described what happened when the government of Quebec, in which he was minister of finance, announced a new tax structure for the mining industry. The mining companies said they couldn't accept those conditions: they would have to close their Quebec operations and go elsewhere; they couldn't possibly survive; the province would lose thousands of jobs, and on and on.

Mr. Kierans and the Lesage government stuck to their guns. The legislation passed, and a day later the same businesses were calling his office to say, "All right, how is this going to work?"

No mines closed. No jobs were lost. There were still profits to be made.

His point was that vested interests will always pressure and threaten dire things to get the best bargain they can. What they really need to know is how much a government means what it says. If they see that their threats can have an effect, they will push harder. If they see that the government refuses to budge from its position, they will accept the laws of the land and get on with business. They exist to make profits and, if they have to obey environmental or safety regulations, then their technicians will find the way to do it.

I was reminded of all this at a breakfast meeting on the subject of pay equity. It was sponsored by the Wm. Mercer company to go over some of the hazards and refinements of instituting pay equity, and was attended by representatives of business, large organizations, women's groups, and government departments.

They were there to learn about the mechanics. Nobody was saying that it couldn't be done or that it was beyond the ability of the human brain to devise a plan that would work out a relationship between employees, whether truck drivers or secretaries or whatever. That is an astonishing change from just a short while ago.

Now, it may be necessary to point out that pay equity is not the same thing as equal pay for equal work. That was an earlier battle when the women's movement had the same learning experience as Mr. Kierans.

It was common in the past for men and women doing exactly the same job to be paid at different rates. And guess which was lower? When women, through their own organizations and through women's caucuses in their unions, began to push for an end to such discrimination, you'd have thought the sky was about to fall. Couldn't be done, we were told. Businesses would go bankrupt. Governments would collapse. It would signal family breakup. Civilization as we know it would come to an end.

But gradually, it *was* done. Laws were enacted to enforce it and it ceased to be an issue.

Of course that wasn't the end of the story. It was still true that jobs typically done by women were—and are—consistently assigned lower rates of pay than men's. If a computer was brought into an office to be operated by a woman, she would be designated as a stenographer and paid accordingly. If the computer was put into the hands of a male employee, he was called a technician or assistant manager and paid at a higher rate of pay.

These are the sort of instances that women's groups refer to as systemic discrimination: at every turn women's work is seen as less worthy and the remuneration is less too. It's as though the thinking has been that women didn't really need or want the same rewards as men, that they were only working for fun, for pin money, for something to do until their white knight would appear and take them away to his castle.

That may be a nice myth for employers to propagate, but the truth is that the 65 percent of women who must work is about the same percentage of men who must work in order for either to stay above the poverty line.

Pressure from women's groups won the appointment some years ago of a study group to look into women's work and wages. The group was chaired by Judge Rosalie Abella. She introduced the term employment equity and recommended changes to enforce the concept of equal pay for jobs of equal value. The term was later shortened to pay equity.

And, of course, the immediate reaction to the proposals was that it could not be done. No way. Measure a truck driver's job (male) against a secretary's (female)? Impossible. Much too complicated. Bankruptcies, end of civilization, etc.

But now, a short while later, historically speaking, I find myself seated at a breakfast meeting to learn the rudiments of putting pay equity into force in businesses, government agencies and other organizations throughout the province. Nobody in the room is arguing that it can't be done or that the sky will fall.

Sometimes we win a few.

And sometimes we go backwards. In the fall of 1995 the newly elected Harris government in Ontario unravelled the legislation on pay equity, chopped back minimum wages and conducted a brutal attack on welfare recipients. Money that would have fed hungry children went instead to the wealthy with tax cuts.

> The sight of Preston Manning [Reform Leader] and Mike Harris doing a joint news conference following close on the heels of the Ontario Tory's election victory is sobering to say the least. It is more evidence that the New Right is a very different political phenomenon.
> Murray Dobbin, Reform Watch

YOU HAD A CHOICE, MR. PRIME MINISTER

In 1993, as Canadians groaned and moaned their way through another income tax return, I suggested we spare a thought for the wealthiest families in the country. It was possible—just possible—that they would have to pay back the debt that they were allowed to accumulate for twenty-one years, thanks to the generosity of Pierre Elliott Trudeau and his Liberal government.

How timely, you might think. What a much-needed stroke against the deficit. What joy this would bring to the budget-balancers in the government! Well, not exactly.

This story starts back in 1967. The Carter Royal Commission on Taxation recommended that Canada follow the practice of most other developed countries, and start taxing capital gains on the *same basis* as income. The Trudeau government went along half-heartedly. They decided in 1972 that, yes, capital gains would be taxed, but at a much lower rate than recommended—only half of what you and I pay for earned income. And then another loophole was added: taxes would not have to be paid right away, but would come due only when capital assets were sold.

There was a stipulation that upon the death of the owner, the estate would have to pay the capital gains tax "on the increased value" of the deceased's holdings.

But the inevitability of death and taxes doesn't seem to apply to the rich the way it does to the rest of us. People with lots of assets could simply pop them into a private trust. The owner might expire but the trust wouldn't: it could live forever. The Trudeau government was aware of this possibility, of course, and firmly decided that eventually wealthy families would have to pay the tax debt they owed to government—*eventually*. Capital gains taxes on assets held in private trusts would have a holiday for twenty-one years. *Then* they would pay their debt.

That time limit was up on January 1, 1993. At the time, I avidly searched the news stories to see whether Michael Wilson's Bill No. 91-018 made it through the House of Commons. The bill, introduced the previous February, would provide another loophole, another delay. This time government wanted to allow family trusts to put off the payment date until the day their youngest child dies. Billions of dollars is owed the government of Canada by the wealthiest citizens in the country, and a reluctant Finance Minister doesn't want to collect it.

It is generally recognized that a dollar of debt deferred is a dollar saved. This is certainly true for the people who would benefit from Wilson's bill. For twenty-one years they had been re-investing and drawing interest on the money they had been allowed to defer paying to the government.

But it works the other way, too. For every dollar given to the rich, the government could long ago have paid off a dollar of our debt load—a debt that would not be there today if the Liberals and the Tories had instituted a fair system of taxation. A system like the one recommended by the Carter Commission.

Now we are being asked to pay the huge deficit that they have both created while allowing their wealthy friends to continue to make fortunes on the money they owe to the treasury.

It's not social programs that racked up the deficit. It is a callous two-tier taxation system that benefits the rich and penalizes the middle and lower classes, and it got an enormous boost in the early seventies. When Trudeau's Liberal government invented this convoluted method for non-payment of capital gains taxes by the wealthiest in Canada, they also eliminated the inheritance tax.

The effect of the two actions was that wealth accumulated up to 1972 that would have been subject to inheritance tax—estimated at $66 billion—actually escaped taxation entirely. One economist has calculated that this meant a lump-sum gift to Canada's wealthiest families of $12 billion. This windfall for the wealthy came to be worth more in subsequent years as the accumulations of wealth reached new heights in Canada during the 1980s.

Remember the words of Brian Mulroney, delivered in 1984 in that low, throaty voice that he used to indicate sincerity? "No, Mr. Prime Minister, you had a choice!" He was heaping scorn on the list of patronage appointments that Pierre Trudeau had handed over to be endorsed by the new Prime Minister, John Turner. A waste of taxpayer's money, Mr. Mulroney thundered, pouring it into the pockets of friends of the Liberal Party.

Well, he was right. Mr. Turner had a choice, and Mr. Trudeau before him had a choice. But Mr. Mulroney also had choices. He could have collected tax money from the thousands of corporations that pay no taxes at all, but instead he gave us the GST. He could have revamped the Income Tax system to make it truly progressive, but instead he cut out the Family Allowance and cut back on transfers to the provinces and insisted that you and I must pay the deficit.

This left little to guess about in the choice he would make about the billions of deferred tax dollars. I guess you knew what would happen. The Bill quietly slipped through and the billions stay buried. Government has no interest in claiming the treasure trove of cash owing this country from its wealthiest citizens.

> ...the $10 billion a year the government needed to reduce the deficit could easily have been raised by tax increases, by closing tax loopholes, and by enacting a wealth tax.
> Neil Brooks, tax expert and law professor,
> Osgoode Hall Law School.

GOVERNMENT IN NORWAY AND RIGHT-WING FROTH

One night in 1988, I watched a fascinating item on CBC television's *Fifth Estate* about Norway's recently-elected Labour government. The woman prime minister, Gro Harlem Bruntland, had appointed a cabinet with equal representation of men and women—seven other women besides herself, and eight men.

Predictably, the leader of the Conservative opposition told Eric Malling that the new prime minister had scandalously put in women cabinet ministers "just because they are women" and ignored many brighter, more able men. When the remark was repeated to her by the interviewer, Prime Minister Brundtland was astonished.

"Did he really say that?" she asked. "He would never make such a statement in Norway. Why would he say it to Canadians? I will ask him to explain himself!"

And you could tell by the glint in her eye that she would, too. I wish I'd been there to hear his answer.

It's funny how that phrase always comes up when women are appointed to anything outside their traditional roles—"just because they are women." The assumption seems to be that the woman is probably incompetent and not possibly the best person for the job. Men, on the other hand, are assumed to be competent for any job, unless proven otherwise. And even when they have given repeated and undeniable proof of incompetence, they are not usually demoted but pushed upstairs. If they were recognized to be incompetent it would reflect unfavourably on the man who appointed them in the first place. It's called the "Peter Principle" (no snickering, please).

What was really rankling with the Conservative opposition leader was that the new government's response to Norway's recession, caused by a falling-off of the North Sea oil bonanza, was to forge ahead with social programs. Housing and other increased benefits for the elderly, strengthening of the health system, a comprehensive program for child care; it seemed that the Norwegian cabinet was bringing a women's perspective to the operation of government.

One appointment that sounded very strange to Canadian ears was of a Commissioner for Children's Rights. There was even a "hot line" that children could call for help if they felt their rights were being violated! As a society we are so unused to taking children seriously that it was almost embarrassing to hear such a thing discussed. But the commissioner's explanation put things in perspective. She said something to the effect that it is essential for children to be treated justly and fairly if they are to be the citizens of a just and fair society in 20 or 30 years.

While still trying to imagine a government that regards proper care for children as an investment in the future, I was brought down to earth with a thump by a news item in *The Evening Telegram*. It was a report of a speech by Conrad Black, one of the wealthiest men in Canada, a man whom prime ministers like to call their friend and advisor.

Speaking to the right-wing Fraser Institute in Vancouver, Mr. Black warned that "Canadians are heading for a showdown with their economy as they try to pay for one of the most expensive social-service systems in the world." He wanted his business friends to help in the delicate process of weaning governments away from excessive social programs.

Poor Mr. Black wants to see more hospital closures, more unemployed, more cuts to medicare and to children and to the elderly, while the corporate class he represents rake in profits that have never been so obscene.

Here in Newfoundland we have already felt for some time the effects of the sort of policies Conrad recommends, but we ain't seen nothing yet from a federal government that is all too willing to follow the Conrad-course. He wants Ottawa to abandon its goal of equalizing economic disparities between provinces because "this drains initiatives."

Of course, he doesn't want to do it all at once. He urges that the cutbacks be made as uncontroversial (i.e. hidden) as possible so that those who promoted them would not be called "ignorant, greedy yahoos." Well, he needn't worry about me. I'd never call him that. I'd call him a clever, knowledgeable, greedy yahoo. And I rather wish someone *would* drain his initiatives.

Now, let's see...I wonder how we could set up a free trade deal with Norway and trade them Conrad Black for Gro Bruntland?

Seven years later, Conrad Black has had most of his wishes granted by the Chrétien Liberal government, and ignorant, greedy yahoos have won a majority in the U.S. Congress. Mr. Black continues to expand his communication empire.

4 The Protection Racket

Today, one of the most health-threatening and environmentally hazardous practices in the Central American region is the continued and elevated use of pesticides and herbicides. Rachel Carson, in her prophetic book *Silent Spring*, was one of the first to warn of the deadly link between pesticides and cancer. Yet, despite the danger, world pesticide production has increased dramatically— from approximately 400,000 tons in 1955 to three million tons in 1985.

    Margarita Penon Arias, President,
    The Arias Foundation for Peace and
    Human Progress,
    speaking to the Women's Environment &
    Development Organization forum, Cairo, 1994.

WOMEN AS GUINEA PIGS

In the early sixties when I was pregnant with my second child I went to my Vancouver doctor for a regular check-up. After the usual examinations and questions, he asked if I was experiencing any nausea. I replied that I was, but that it was no problem and lasted for only a short period each morning.

He said, "Well, you don't need to have that," and dug into a drawer to hand over a sample package of pills. I reiterated that I was not complaining, that I was as healthy as could be, that the nausea was very slight and that I did not need any medication. The doctor repeated that I did not need to have any nausea at all, pushed the pills across his desk and advised me to take them.

My mother was a nurse who had enormous respect for the taking of pills, any pills. I don't think I even saw aspirin in our house when I was growing up. Medicine was only used for severe illness under strict orders from the doctor. There was no idle handing out of pills for any of the usual aches or pains. Her attitude rubbed off on me and I bless her for it. I took home the pills the doctor had given me, put them in the back of the medicine cupboard and forgot all about them.

Shortly after our beautiful baby was born, we read about the tragic births across Canada of dozens of babies without arms or legs, deformities caused by the drug Thalidomide, a tranquillizer that had been prescribed for pregnant women in Canada from April, 1961, until March, 1962, to relieve nausea, vomiting and insomnia.

I rushed to the medicine cabinet and with a chill of horror learned that the samples the doctor had pushed on me were one of the brands of that ghastly drug. I'll never forgive him for the damage he could have done.

All of this was brought vividly back to mind by a recent article in *The Evening Telegram* telling the shocking story of members of the Canadian armed forces being fully aware of the dreadful effect of Thalidomide long before the drug was allowed to be sold in Canada. The man telling the story is Clifford Chadderton, chief executive officer of the War Amputations of Canada. He felt the time had come to unburden himself and was quoted as saying, "If the army hadn't been so insular in its views as to its responsibility, it could have instigated an investigation that would have stopped Thalidomide dead in its tracks (in Canada)."

In the late 1950s, some fifteen severely deformed children were born to wives of Canadian servicemen stationed in West Germany. Mr. Chadderton was sent secretly to Germany to decide the fate of the children. Sadly, the parents were told they must leave them behind because there were no proper facilities in Canada to care for them. The German authorities had already set up facilities to deal with their own epidemic of Thalidomide babies and Canadian babies could be quietly added to the group. But the military officials did nothing to warn public health authorities in this country.

Dr. Frances Kelsey of the U.S. Health Department was a hero to women in her country for stopping Thalidomide before it could be distributed. But Canadian officials holding the same documentation allowed the drug companies to distribute it and freely give it out, even as samples.

Feminists have devoted a lot of time and research to the subject of health, demonstrating that all too often women have been guinea pigs for the pharmaceutical industry with the active cooperation of some doctors. It is well known that for years women have been over-prescribed tranquillizers to "keep them calm." There is ample evidence that some doctors treat women's symptoms as unimportant and casually prescribe drugs, while similar symptoms from a man get full-scale medical examination to see where the problem lies. Women are challenging the medical profession and the health care system and making some progress but the abuses never stop coming.

The drug Stilbestrol, or as it is more commonly known—DES, was given to pregnant women in the 1940s, 50s, and 60s, to prevent miscarriages. It is a synthetic hormone that has been found to produce, in some cases, cancer in the offspring of the mother who took it and sometimes other abnormalities. It has come under attack from women's organizations and is now banned (for all but one medical use) in Western countries, but it is still being prescribed to women in Third World countries.

The Women's Press publication, *Adverse Effects, Women and the Pharmaceutical Industry*, documents the sorry history of DES and other experimental drugs. Carcinogenic warnings dating back to 1938 didn't prevent the government from allowing DES on the Canadian market in 1947. The history of DES once again illustrates the callous lack of concern for the protection of pregnant women and their infants both from the huge profit-making industry and our own health authorities.

In July of 1995, we were very close to another health risk when it appeared that government authorities would cave in to Monsanto and Eli Lilly and allow them to bring the drug, BST, or Synthetic Bovine Somatotropin, into Canada.

The chemical companies claim the product has no significant effect on milk but that farmers can use it to increase milk production. Canadian farmers point out that there is already a surplus in milk supply and that injected cows in the U.S. have developed mastitis and other illnesses and die at an earlier age than normal.

The effect of this hormone on humans is unknown and worrisome.

> There is concern that an insulin-like growth factor—known as IGF-1—in biosynthetic milk may be a risk factor in breast and gastrointestinal cancers.
> Women's Network on Health and The Environment.

Word was spread by farmers, health and consumer groups and organizations like The Council of Canadians, who organized tens of thousands of petitions to be sent to Ottawa. Eventually word came that further studies would be done.

New Zealand and Australia have banned BST totally, and the European Union have clamped a moratorium on it until at least the year 2000. It bears watching.

A NATIONAL DISGRACE

In April, 1991, Health and Welfare Canada announced it would take the Meme breast implant off the market. Big deal! The news announcement came shortly after the manufacturer had "voluntarily" pulled the device from the world market. The impression was left that government jumped in to protect us just as soon as they heard of this surprising "precautionary" move. That may sound reassuring but it doesn't fit with the facts.

According to other sources, Health and Welfare had known for a long time that this device was dangerous to women. The April, 1991 issue of *Saturday Night* gave the story in dismal detail. Far from being a protective agency, the department is condemned in the article's title as a "National Disgrace."

It's not us that has been protected, Nicholas Regush demonstrates; it's the industries who have manufactured faulty equipment, including infant incubators, tampons, surgical gloves, dialysis machines, heart valves and this awful breast implant. He suggests that if we believe our watchdog agency is working on our behalf then we probably also believe in the tooth fairy.

One of the few good guys to emerge from the story is Dr. Pierre Blais, described by a director as "the most brilliant scientist who ever worked for me." In the mid-1980s Dr. Blais read disquieting information that the foam coating designed to keep the Meme breast implant soft had been found to break up and decompose after a period of time in the body. From that moment on, he kept a watching brief on the implant, collecting all relevant material.

Dr. Blais was employed at the time in the Bureau of Medical Devices, a division of the National Health Protection Branch, and in 1988 he published his misgivings about the Meme implant. He later learned that the foam coating had been developed for industrial use and had never been intended for medical purposes. Experiments on animals were showing that a chemical called 2,4-Toluene diamine was a byproduct of the decomposed foam and is a suspected cancer-causing agent.

In January, 1989, Dr. Blais and six of his fellow scientists asked the

Bureau to request the manufacturer, Surgitek of Racine, Wisconsin, to voluntarily remove the implant from the market until its safety could be documented. The Health Bureau declined. Over 12,000 Canadian women had already received the implant, but in spite of the worrisome evidence that something was badly wrong, the department decided not to follow the advice of its scientists. The Meme implant was left on the market and the manufacturer was simply asked to submit safety data. No warning was sent to doctors, nor to women across Canada.

Sadly, less than a quarter of implants were done because of losing a breast after having a mastectomy. Eighty percent of the cases were for "cosmetic" reasons. It is a tragic commentary that women have risked their lives to live up to the images of *Playboy*, believing that their human worth had something to do with the size of their breasts. And it's hard to believe that there would be doctors willing to encourage them. It's equally clear that no such operation nor indignity would ever be suggested to men. Their physical dimensions are simply accepted as a part of their own integrity.

Dr. Blais wrote strong recommendations to his superiors in January of 1989, calling for the implant to be removed from the market. His words were altered and edited in a formal document, orders were given to destroy his memo, and—too depressingly familiar—pressure came from all sides to silence him until he was finally fired in July of that year.

In February, 1992, the Chairman of Dow Corning, John Ludington, stepped down. The implant issue was cited as a reason for the change. The record showed that the company had known for decades that the implants were hazardous.

We Canadians are and have been a trusting race. We've assumed that governments and their departments work on our behalf. We've assumed that products wouldn't be allowed on the market until they were proven safe. We've believed that our governments make sure that food and drugs are free of poisonous materials, and we've never doubted that medical devices had to be safe before hospitals could use them. We've wanted to believe that, but if we still do it's in spite of the evidence.

A whole collection of new laboratory techniques are now being used on women under the heading of New Reproductive Technologies. They are fraught with danger, and a Royal Commission was set up to look into the implications.

If there was honest political will to protect women's health, the people who have allowed this industrial foam to be placed in women's breasts would be out on the street tomorrow, if not in jail, and Dr. Blais would be the new Minister of Health.

BOYCOTTS AND BUFFALOES

The April, 1989 issue of the *New Internationalist* was entitled "How To Help Children." The magazine claimed that "in the last twenty-four hours about 40,000 children died—over 80% of them from preventable diseases ...measles, whooping cough, tetanus... Every year there are around fourteen million child deaths in the Third World—mainly of children under five."

Malnutrition is often the basic cause of death and other crippling diseases. A quarter of a million children go blind because they lack vitamin A. Mothers die from conditions that could easily be prevented, leaving a million children behind, many of whom end up living on the streets in the major centres of Third World countries.

I had noticed the boycott on Nestle's products (and American Home Products) was back again and the reasons seem to be about the same as those in the past. Millions of poor women in Third World countries are being persuaded by high-pressure advertising to bottle-feed their babies. The precious proteins and antibodies found in breast milk are denied to these infants. In poor areas of the Third World, bottle-fed babies are twice as likely to die as breast-fed ones.

Another positive feature of breast feeding lies in the fact that it also prevents more births than all other forms of birth control put together, because it inhibits menstruation, so that breast-feeding mothers not only have healthier babies, they also have fewer of them.

Some time ago, I had the good fortune to hear an address by Elinor Ratcliffe, a native of St. John's home for a visit. She was speaking to the gentlemen of the Golden K Club. Elinor and her husband have been prime movers in supporting family planning clinics in different parts of the world. Much of what she described of her own experiences and observations confirmed the information in the *New Internationalist*—the homeless families, the abandoned children, the disease and malnutrition.

But her talk had its lighter moments, too, especially when she told of a family planning program instituted by the government of Thailand. She described a clinic where men go voluntarily to have vasectomies. While they are resting afterwards, in a manner reminiscent of a blood donor clinic, they are entertained by groups of little boys and girls who come in singing songs to thank them for their contribution to a rational world.

It is very difficult for me, as a woman and a Canadian, to imagine what effect that might have on the patients, but if it encourages the Thai male we might want to consider it. The men are further rewarded by the Thai government by being allowed to rent water buffaloes at a low price. As the huge buffalo toils in the farmer's field, it wears a sandwich board over its back proclaiming to the world, "I had a vasectomy."

Now that's something you don't see every day. Nor, come to think of it, do we often see men's clubs inviting feminists to speak to them on such delicate issues of common concern. It's a courageous step, and one that should be rewarded, or at least recognized. I wonder if the Golden K could use a water buffalo?

Whenever things get tough in our country we see a rash of letters in daily papers decrying Canada's contribution to Third World countries, as though the children and adults dying in the streets had nothing to do with us. But the fact is that their poverty and our wealth are both part of a global economic system. We use Third World Countries as sources of raw material and cheap labour, and as markets for our excess production.

This global system has allowed us to use most of the world's resources at an appalling rate, and in the process we have caused havoc for all living creatures. We have polluted the water, air, and land. Even the ozone layer that protects us from the sun is threatened by our insatiable demand for consumer goods. Obviously, we cannot continue this way. And as Elinor Ratcliffe pointed out, even if all we cared about was our own survival, we would have to be committed to finding the solutions.

AN APPLE A DAY

A friend was telling us about her experiences from a few months in Portugal with her husband and ten-month-old baby. She used a phrase that is always pleasant for parents to hear, even if their own children are grown up: "They love children." And then she added, "Everywhere you go in Portugal, children are welcomed and looked after."

We've all heard that said about some other countries too. But Canada? I wonder if visitors in our country would go away with similar memories? They would, of course, meet lots of individuals who would shower children with affection. But what about our institutions?

I was reminded of all this as I listened to *Quirks and Quarks* on CBC Radio, and later *The Food Show*. They were discussing the horrific situation that has been allowed to develop: the beautiful apples in our supermarkets and those countless cans of apple juice which we buy for our children have been carrying cancer-causing chemicals.

All this time, we've been encouraging our children to eat nice, healthy apples instead of candy that will rot their teeth. We've encouraged nice, healthy apple juice instead of soft drinks loaded with sugar or artificial sweeteners. In some big, wicked cities there were people who put pins or razor blades in apples at Halloween, but they were isolated maniacs who needed to be caught and locked up.

And all the while the apple industry, with the cooperation of our government, has been spraying apples with a poison that is aimed directly at our children. Children are 250 times more vulnerable to this cancer-causing agent than are adults. It is called Alar, one of the many chemicals sprayed on apple crops. The growers like it because it keeps apples on the tree. They don't fall off before they're picked. Alar attracted a lot of attention when U.S. studies led the American government finally to forbid its use.

At first it was good to hear that B.C. Apple Growers have refused since last year to distribute any apples from growers who use the chemical. But the pleasure paled somewhat when the spokesperson for the B.C. industry gave the reason why they had taken that stand. Proudly, he pointed out that their organization had discussed the chemical and then decided against the use of it "because we felt the bad publicity would be worse than having the apples fall to the ground."

On *Quirks and Quarks* there was an interview with a woman from the department of our own federal government that deals with food and drug protection. Incredibly, in the face of the U.S. evidence, she defended Canada's lack of concern and assured us that there was no reason to be alarmed. A U.S. scientist came on after her and tore her arguments to pieces. "There is no safe level of carcinogenic substances," he said. "You are dealing with a loaded gun, and you are playing Russian roulette with the lives of children. All apples sprayed with this pesticide contain the poison. It goes completely through the entire apple and is present in the juice as well as the fruit. No washing can get rid of it."

Of course, this particular chemical is just one of many that have worrisome hazards. Dr. Willard of the Canadian Medical Association pointed out that our federal agency doesn't even test for over 60 percent of the chemicals that are sprayed on produce sold in Canadian markets. He said that, basically, our Department of Health—the agency we depend on to protect us—accepts the data from the manufacturers, and he added, "Very often it is falsified."

Canada's unwillingness to accept the findings of the U.S. study are grimly reminiscent of the days when the same department and our parliament allowed Thalidomide to be prescribed for pregnant women.

To go back to the original question, is this a country where children are loved? I think that most of us would like it to be. But you sure couldn't tell it from the way our governments allow our "protection" agencies to operate.

MIDWIVES' TALES

A woman stopped me one day to tell about the birth of her newborn. She was bubbling over with happiness at the whole miraculous experience, but had stopped me particularly because a friend of mine had acted as her midwife.

It meant so much to her to have the support of this kind and wise woman who apparently kept her in gales of laughter through the whole thing, even in the tense moments. I'm not sure that it was necessary for this wonderful midwife to go blabbing about the funny things that go on around our bridge table. Still, if it eased the delivery—and I'm told that it did—then I'll have to forgive the indiscretions.

I've known many others who have sung similar praises of this nurse, and I must admit that I sometimes envy the women she helps. How pleasant it must be to share the excitement of a growing pregnancy with a knowledgeable and sympathetic women who can answer your questions, allay your fears and share your exultation right up to and including the birth.

It's hard to understand why Canada has been one of the few remaining countries in the world that hasn't recognized midwifery as a part of the health care system. But that is changing. Ontario's decision to legalize midwifery was very good news. It is no accident that the cabinet minister who prepared the legislation is a woman. And, what's more, is a woman who cares about these things. When she announced the bill, she told of her own unhappy experiences in the hospital system when her children were born and of how she had vowed then, like so many other women, to make it better for others. At times like this, I am reminded of the question that is asked of me regularly, "But why will electing, or appointing, or training, or hiring women make a difference?"

Incredibly, the practice of obstetrics has been almost entirely in the hands of men. If there is one branch of medicine that you would have thought should go first to women it is surely maternity, but that has not been the case. Things would have been very different if it had. For one thing, I don't think midwives would have been lost to the system. And I don't think some of the barbaric indignities would have become the norm, the ones that are a convenience to the doctor and a distress to the mother and child, such as stirrups and drugs and being shaved.

A book entitled *A Midwife's Story* by Penny Armstrong and Sheryle Feldman gives a fascinating account of one midwife's experiences in two very different circumstances.

In a Glasgow hospital, Armstrong says "form ranked above everything else, including the well-being of mother and child." Although the hospital served a poor area and was in other ways inadequately equipped, "every last obstetric gadget in the modern world is automatically hooked up to a woman having a baby." As a result, the whole experience is completely depersonalized: "when the doctors come to check a woman, they do not look at her, ask her questions, or feel her belly: they read the graph paper coming out of her machine."

The author does not condemn the proper use of medical technology, but she does condemn a philosophy that puts technology in charge rather than enhancing the human abilities that are natural to childbirth.

The Glaswegian women Penny Armstrong was dealing with had no control over their own lives: they fought an endless, losing battle against poverty, ignorance, and brutality. The delivery room, the one place where money is spent lavishly on their behalf, is just another reflection of the total control that other people had over their lives. Her later experiences in Pennsylvania stand in vivid contrast. There, among the prosperous Amish farmers, childbirth was treated as part of the natural cycle.

Our first child was born in the traditional way, at the traditional inconvenient hour, in hospital: father banished to the waiting room to pace, mother taken away, fortunately dilating, so that it was too late for much of the shaving or drugging techniques. And in the morning the drill began: 5:30, wake up to wash; 6:30, baby brought in to nurse; 7:30, breakfast;

8:30, doctor says hello. By 9:00, I thought I had put in a full day, but that was nothing compared to the tremendous loss I felt at not being able to have my baby with me all day. Everyone was kind enough. It was just that mother and child had to fit into the day's routines. That was what was important.

I recalled the lecture that my husband and I had attended the month before. Dr. Brock Chisholm, speaking for the United Nations World Health Organization, was focusing on the world population problem. It was not the most comfortable topic for a woman in my condition; I never felt so huge and pregnant. In the course of the talk he spoke of Asian countries he had visited where the child lies in a small hammock at the foot of the mother's bed and is lulled to sleep, with the mother gently rocking the wee bed with her foot.

All that was at a time when people in Canada believed that our spiffy new hospitals, full of equipment, were the best things that could be offered to expectant mothers. But in hospital I realized that some major considerations had been left out. I hungered for my child to be with me. I didn't want him to be an occasional visitor. I wanted his father to hold him, not view him through a window. I wanted to feed my son when he wanted, not when it suited the system.

In spite of the hassles, it was still a wonderful experience. My husband shared it as best he could by getting violently ill in a movie house the night before I delivered, so that we had to take him home and put him to bed. We never did find out how the movie ended. Six hours later we headed to hospital.

When the next one was about to be born, my husband was struck with a toothache, after never having had one in his entire life. We were out canvassing for our favourite political party and the poor man nearly crawled back to the car with the pains that were suddenly shooting through his head.

There was nothing wrong with his teeth. The dentist hammered every one of them while I gave birth in the maternity ward to our second son. My husband's sympathy symptoms were impressive, but not for an anthropologist. There's a tribe of people who do it even better. The man lies down and has actual contractions while his wife does the delivering.

By the time of my second confinement I had got smarter. I had learned that there was something called "rooming in," and although the Vancouver General Hospital was not really allowing this, we managed to find a doctor who helped us make the arrangements. This meant there would be no silly appointments with washcloths, no needless preparations for doctor's visits, but best of all I had my child with me.

I know this arrangement isn't preferred by all women—and if it was my sixth I might have thought differently—but it suited me down to the ground. We melded our timetables together and I could enjoy just watching him sleep or twitch and his father could hold him for hours.

Our third child was the most momentous, in some ways, because she is adopted. For her arrival, mother and father were on equal ground. We both lay awake for the three nights we had to wait after seeing her for the first time, counting the minutes until we could carry her home with us. We shall hold forever the wonder of being allowed to be her parents.

The point is that women need to be able to make their own choices and have alternatives presented to them. A woman giving birth should not be treated as a cog in the machinery but as an intelligent human being who has a vested interest in how her baby comes into the world. Doctors tend to talk about delivering your baby. Midwives don't. They say the woman delivers the baby; they are there to catch it.

Canada is at last getting into the act. Ontario was the first to pass legislation recognizing midwifery as part of the health-care system. Alberta and British Columbia followed, and other provinces are moving in that direction.

5 Vive la Difference

I was once on a CBC radio panel with the Honourable Minister for the Status of Women, Patt Cowan, who spoke for the Liberal party, And the Honourable Lynn Verge, MHA, who represented the Conservatives. I represented the New Democratic Party. The topic was "Why aren't more women getting elected?"

My husband said later that we would all three probably be drummed out of our respective parties because we didn't play the game. In the first place we kept agreeing with each other and then instead of interrupting kept ensuring that the other had a turn. Not like true politicians at all, he said.

It may sound funny but it was a demonstration of the kind of differences that women could bring to politics.

WOMEN FOR THE BURNING

"It's going to be a new church on March 12 [1994]," said Deacon Berners-Wilson, the first woman to become a priest in the Church of England. After 19 years of debate close to a thousand women would finally be ordained as priests in Britain over a period of three months.

The church was in turmoil. In Sheffield, twenty-five women deacons were lined up and waiting for their moment in history. The Bishop of Sheffield refused to conduct their ordination services, so another Bishop had to take his place.

Traditionalists have warned that a thousand angry male priests may very well leave the Church of England in disgust. Many of them are expected to transfer their allegiance to the Roman Catholic faith. No one has mentioned the possibility, but I wonder if this exodus will be balanced by a lot of Catholic women joining the Church of England?

The most startling expression of anger came from the Reverend Anthony Kennedy of Lincolnshire. The *Globe and Mail* (March 10, 1994) quoted him as saying that women priests are "bloody bitches who should be burned at the stake—like medieval witches."

His remarks to reporters were apparently to remind the populace that he had said on many occasions that he would "burn the bitches" or happily "shoot the bastards. Let these bloody women go off and form their own politically correct church and religion," he said. His Bishop apologized for the vicar's outburst, sent him a letter of rebuke, and called him on the carpet to explain himself.

It would be interesting to know what the explanation might consist of. It seems to me that the vicar explained himself with abundant clarity. Probably what the Bishop really needs is a run-down of what other colourful messages Mr. Kennedy may have delivered from his pulpit. What'll you bet that at the Vatican the public relations department is screening calls from Lincolnshire?

At the other end of the scale, the Bishop of Bristol happily conducted the first service for ordination of thirty-two women, with Ms Berners-Wilson leading the way. "C'mon in and join the queue," she said to visitors. "Every time the phone rings it's another reporter." And well they might be lining up for interviews.

This historic event ended 460 years of male-only tradition and will change the church significantly. It's enough to rattle the bones of Henry VIII. I've no idea how many Anglican priests there are in England, but I do know that the introduction of a thousand women within a few months is an unparalleled victory for women.

This is not your usual case of a few token women being added gradually to the profession. It far outshines Canada's record in spite of the fact that the Anglican Church here was years ahead of Britain in allowing women to be priests. The British coup has outstretched them all and produced a landslide. It opens up wonderful opportunities. A thousand women can take inspiration and strength from each other and introduce new ideas to combat old ones. They can meet and network. Just by being there they demonstrate a powerful message to youth.

These women will likely remember that their progress was not individual but a result of many women's work. And I'm sure they'll see themselves as linked to the thousand courageous women who sat in British jails to get the vote and who changed the public climate for women's eventual acceptance.

A thousand women priests invading the pulpits of Britain are bound to make a difference: to remind us that the basis of religion lies in sharing, not in maintaining law and order to enrich the powerful. One of the new priestly recruits has warned that "the ordination of women is just the beginning of reform." To which one can only add a hearty, "Amen."

WHEN ALL ELSE FAILS
Or: A Month in the Life of Women Activists

February 22, 1990: Red Alert! Red Alert! Women's centres across Canada slashed from Secretary of State operational funding. Eighty centres endangered. Project funding to be cut next year and every year after.

This is not a drill. Repeat, this is not a drill. All women report to Action Stations...

Where to begin? Proper channels, of course: Minister of Secretary of State, Gerry Weiner. Mary Collins, Status of Women. Two St. John's Tory MPs, Ross Reid, John Crosbie.

Strange, nobody can speak in person. Messages accepted by staff. Letters sent. Faxes faxed.

Opposition members speak in person, no problem.

Feb. 23: Public must be informed. St. John's Women's Centre holds press conference. Main message: "Help!"

Feb. 28: Women, men, rally on steps of Atlantic Place. Speeches spoken, songs sung, placards waved.

March 3: Women, men, stand on street corners, ask passersby to sign cards to send to government. Cold. Windy. Most people sign. Start of International Women's Week. Meetings all week.

March 14: Wendy Williams, President of Provincial Advisory Council on the Status of Women, in Ottawa, meeting other advisories. Special meeting with Minister Weiner set up by Ross Reid, MP. Nice Fellow. In bad company, though.

Minister Weiner friendly, reassuring. Things not so bad. Will be more flexible. Good word, flexibility.

March 16-19: Whoops. Reassurance mistaken. Government has no intention to budge on operational funding cuts. This is flexible?

More posters. Phone calls. Strangers drop in at Women's Centre, leave money, say "hang in there." Artist donates two paintings for fundraising. Good man.

Women talk to newspapers, radio, television. Explain role of Women's Centres. Tell how every government dollar matched by $100.00 of volunteer service. Operational funding crucial to maintaining key services.

More phone calls. Can't get through to government MPs for St. John's East and St. John's West. Strange.

Opposition MPs willing to talk, though. Not so strange. Some even willing to listen.

March 21: News flash! Stop press! Private member's bill by MHA Percy Barrett in support of Women's Centres gets unanimous approval in Newfoundland House of Assembly! How come MHAs so much smarter than MPs?

Maybe Atlantic wind blowing fresh air in brains. Maybe could be packaged for sale. Idea for Economic Recovery Commission.

March 22: Big meeting in Pleasantville. Representatives of supporting organizations, ordinary citizens, women, men. Local politicians of all stripes lend support and urge women to stick with it. Nice feeling.

March 23-25: Time running out. Strategy meetings around clock. Proper channels not working. Time to be improper? Decision: Yes.

March 26: New Women's Centre located on eighth floor of Atlantic Place. Used to be called offices of Secretary of State. Nice place. Would make dandy daycare centre.

Women and men march around offices, carrying signs. Sing songs. Tell non-sexist jokes. Say things like "Maybe we should have a Weiner roast." Oh, dear. Maybe not so non-sexist after all. Laugh anyway.

People of all political shades among the occupiers, including Tory MHAs Lynn Verge and Shannie Duff. Lynn uses liberated telephone, tries to reach Minister Weiner to explain extreme measures. Gets assistant to assistant. Leaves impassioned message.

Liberal women get promise from MP Marian Catteral to put question in House of Commons. NDP MP Margaret Mitchell promises to give full statement in House.

Advisory Council reports full support for Women's centres from four Atlantic premiers meeting in Corner Brook. Each one will send urgent request to Prime Minister. If women can get Atlantic premiers to agree on something, anything possible.

Assistant to Minister Weiner returns Lynn Verge's call. Lynn and Shannie gone to House of Assembly, but Minister's assistant gets full report. Takes a while to understand local emergency situation, but promises to inform Minister.

Copy of press release from Ross Reid's office, telling press but not women-sit-downers of possible meeting. Rather vague on details.

End of working day. Firemen show proper emergency exits, get colouring books for children. Women unroll sleeping bags, prepare to spend the night.

March 27: Occupation continues. Phone lines burning up. Open Line Host Andy Wells carries on live interview with occupiers on morning phone-in program. So does Host Bill Rowe on other station, is serenaded with original lyrics all about peace, justice and equality.

Doctor from city hospital comes in with petition of support signed by 101 hospital workers who know at first hand the value of Women's Centres. Reads petition on radio.

Flash! Letter from John Crosbie MP offering support! No mention of Sheila Copps or Mexican alcoholic beverage.

Double flash! Message from Minister Weiner. Personal representative to fly to St. John's tonight to meet with protesters. Is given address for meeting: Atlantic Place, 8th. floor. Cautioned to step carefully over sleeping children.

March 28: 12:01 a.m: Damn! Press deadline time. And this won't appear until Saturday! All sorts of things could have happened by then!

All sorts of things did happen: Women occupied the offices for four nights and five days. Funding was eventually restored for women's centres across Canada. In the spring of 1995, at a Buddy Wassisname concert, the man sitting next to my husband recognized me and began to talk about the occupation. His girlfriend had been one of the occupation forces, and he had helped out with food and support. He remembers the events vividly, and feels that we need a similar spirit today to protect other social programs.

INSPIRATION FROM THE WOMEN OF ERITREA

In many of the poorer countries of the world, the mass of the people do not have even the most basic civil and human rights. And in most of them, women bear a double burden, oppressed both by autocratic governments and by patriarchal cultures that define women as inferior.

Nowhere has that been more true than in Eritrea. "Just as there is no donkey with horns," says an Eritrean proverb,"so there is no woman with brains." Women were treated worse than donkeys. As youngsters of two years, little girls underwent a brutal operation on their genitals called infibulation, intended to prevent sexual intercourse until they were *married property* at which time a second operation would be called for. Some died as a result, and many were left with chronic infections.

They received no formal education and were forced into marriages as early as age 11 to men who might already have several wives. They could own no property and their husbands could divorce them at will. As wives they were servants to their husbands. In factories they were paid half the wages given to men for the same work. It goes without saying that they had no influence on political decisions.

It is hard to believe that a women's liberation movement could gain a foot-hold in such an environment, but apparently it has. A remarkable article by Blaine Harden of the *Washington Post*, reprinted in the Toronto Star, tells the story of how some women are revolutionizing the ancient patriarchal society.

The sad irony is that the advances they have wrought have come about through their involvement in another ancient male pastime—warfare. In the seemingly endless 26-year Ethiopian civil war, as in every other aspect of the society, women bore some of the heaviest suffering. Harden quotes Lel Ghebreab, Chairperson of the National Union of Eritrean Women as saying:

> In Europe and America, women are well fed, their children are safe. They demand such things as nuclear disarmament. For us, there are more immediate concerns. Most women went into the struggle because we faced atrocities. Women are living in caves, always afraid that the enemy would come and rape them, kill them and kill their children. We agitated the men, asking, "Is it better for us to die in the village or go out and fight?"

The men of the Eritrean People's Liberation Front (EPLF) resisted, but they needed fighters. In the early 1970s a few women were given special military and political training and allowed to go into battle. According to Ghebreab, eventually 30 per cent of the EPLF fighting forces were women. And one in every three casualties was a woman.

Almost immediately after they began to fight, she says, women "began agitating and doing political work." The National Union of Eritrean Women became an arm of the rebel movement and began to work at transforming the society. "When a woman proved herself a successful fighter at the front," Ghebreab said, "she could go back to her village with authority. Men had to listen to her. She could influence other women."

Women of the EPLF were forbidden from entering into the traditional polygamous marriages and from allowing their daughters to undergo the traditional genital operation. In the EPLF schools, boys and girls received the same education.

The women are determined to hold onto the gains that they have made and are engaging in educational programs aimed at eliminating the practices that have kept them in virtual slavery. "We are not just changing our role in society," Harden quotes Ghebreab as saying. "We are changing the roles of the new generation."

It is heart-breaking to think that these women have been forced to take up rifles and machine guns to protect themselves and their children in a senseless struggle over power. But there is also inspiration in the way they have used this dreadful situation to build a society based on equality.

The practice of genital mutilation has been carried out in many countries, including Canada. In 1992 the province of Ontario passed a law forbidding medical doctors to practice genital mutilation when requested by Islamic (or other) fundamentalists who have come to Canada, and in 1995 Québec made the practice illegal. The World Health Organization estimates that 75 million women have suffered this cruelty.

THE BARD WAS A MALE CHAUVINIST

Every year, people the world over celebrate the memory of Robbie Burns, Scotland's national bard. My husband and I, for many years, have celebrated at the home of friends who provide the annual occasion for a group of guests to eat our fill of haggis—which doesn't take long, pay honour to the bard in solemn toasts and pass his collected works from hand to hand for readings in thick (and mostly bad) Scottish accents.

The formal part of the festivities ends with each guest delivering their own piece of prose or verse—not always terribly serious—drawing on some theme from Robbie Burns' work. There is much music, singing of sentimental Scottish ballads, much laughter and, as the Scots would put it, a wee dram or two. Robbie himself would enjoy it, I'm sure.

One of the reasons for Burns' enduring popularity is his common touch. He wrote in the language of the ordinary people of his time and place, and his poetry is full of concern for humanity. But a modern feminist can't help noticing that he was, to put it fairly mildly, pretty much a male chauvinist.

To say that is not to attack what the Scots call "the immortal memory." Burns was the product of a male chauvinist society, where a man could spend much of his life in late-night revelry and promiscuous affairs with milkmaids and be admired for it, while a woman, if she were to have any respect at all, kept quiet, kept the house, and minded the children.

One cannot help but think that there could have been a lot of female contemporaries of Robbie Burns who had as much wit, as much love of life, as much sympathy for human suffering, and as much of a sense of fun as he had. But if they existed we never heard about them. Women were simply not expected to give voice to their thoughts and feelings in literary form. The few who did were regarded as prodigies—on a par, as Samuel Johnson put it in slightly different context—with a dog walking on its hind legs: the wonder was not that they did it well, but that they did it at all.

Things have changed a lot in 200 years, but it is interesting to note that women are still at some disadvantage in literary pursuits. In 1979 the *New York Times* reported on a trend that was showing up in literary journals where published pieces were printed without the author's name. It was a scheme designed to avoid the biased judgement that readers, both male and female, were inclined to make of submissions by women.

That may sound like paranoia, but the bias was vividly demonstrated by a study among university students. Two groups of women students each received a booklet of essays. The essays in each booklet were exactly the same, but for one group the author was listed as John T. McKay, and for the other as Joan T. McKay. The students who read "John's" essays consistently rated them higher in all areas than the students who read "Joan's". One letter in the name made the difference. And, please note, it wasn't male students putting down the female author, it was women. We are all the products of our society.

The women's movement is trying to remake our society. We can't—and shouldn't—rewrite history, but nonetheless it is fun to speculate about what might have happened if a female poet had lived the reckless, rowdy life of Robbie Burns. One thing is sure: she would never have become the national poet of the Scots or anybody else.

So here's to her if she ever existed:

>Now let us honour Robert Burns
>As honoured he must surely be.
>But think how things might have turned out
>If Scotland's bard had been a she.
>
>Her accent would have been as dense,
>Her chest, perhaps, not quite as flat;
>And she might have given a different sense
>To "A man's a man for a' that"!
>
>Poor Robbie suffered more than most
>From pious church-folk who, in detail,
>Condemned the sort of life he led
>But imagine if he'd been a female!
>
>If *she* had wandered Scottish glens
>When springtime had enthralled her,
>Seducing simple farmer lads—
>Now, what would they have called her?
>
>And if she'd stayed out every night
>In boozy celebration
>Would she now be the honoured bard
>Beloved of the Scottish nation?
>
>Yes, Robbie was a charming rogue
>But here I will assert, a
>Nother name we'd have for her,
>If she'd been called Roberta.

A BANK FOR WOMEN?

If there is one subject that comes up repeatedly in every committee of the women's movement it is the financial inequality faced by women. It's well recognized by now that the two largest poverty groups in Canada are older women and single mothers. And it is equally well recognized that this is no accident, but the inevitable result of two main factors. Women as homemakers are a large unpaid labour force, and women in the work environment are subject to discriminatory wages.

What the feminist movement has been striving to do is to bring more security into women's lives, to open up opportunity, to break with traditions that have kept women helpless and vulnerable. Whether you are female or male, if you haven't access to money you are severely limited in what you can do. I've sat in on conferences where women have talked at length about some of the economic development plans that they would like to pursue in their communities. Each speaker always comes back to the fact that they don't stand a ghost of a chance borrowing even small sums of money for any venture, no matter how promising.

Governments don't put these women on their loan boards where changes might be made. Banks and even credit unions don't give loans to the poor.

But a story in the *Manchester Guardian* (April 30, 1989) by Roland-Pierre Paringaux shows how wrong this attitude is. Impoverished Bangladesh has been operating a successful and imaginative banking program that could teach us some lessons. The Grameen Bank has specialized in lending money to the poor, which has made enormous difference in the lives of many people. It has also advanced funds for local projects, for example a pilot project in the village of Suruj Tangail where it has funded a school next door to the bank. Trade skills are taught there, as well as reading and writing. But these are not just your standard aid projects. What is really remarkable is that it is also a highly successful banking operation because of the unusually high rate of repayment.

"Grameen" means "rural," and the bank is the result of the dedicated work of an economics professor determined to prove that bankers are wrong in denying funds to the poor. He developed a scheme to give landless peasants the chance to buy income-generating equipment in order to escape the clutches of moneylenders and middlemen.

The loans are all tiny. For example, enough for a mother of six to earn a cash income for the first time by setting up her own equipment for polishing rice. She doesn't earn much by our standards, but it's a lot more attractive than her previous income of a bowl of rice and a little meat from the merchant for a full day's work. Or a taxi driver who was able to borrow the equivalent of an average year's wages to buy his new cycle-rickshaw, the first he had ever owned.

The system works by having five prospective borrowers organized into a group. They meet regularly with a bank employee to learn how the system operates and to give each other support. At the start, only two people in the group can borrow; when their debt is repaid over a 50-week period, the others then have credit and can apply for their loans.

The bank opened in 1982 and soon had 100 branches serving half a million people. By 1988 it had grown to 500 branches and was expected to double that number in the next few years. What has staggered the banking community is the fact that they have experienced a loan repayment rate of 98 percent. The contrast is marked by a news report from the *Los Angeles Times* which estimated that only 10 percent of the 500 million pounds lent to Bangladesh by the World Bank was ever repaid. Middlemen, consultants and corruption had eaten up the rest.

The success of "the penny bank" is attributed to the operation being run by local, highly motivated people who had worked in the fields themselves, but more especially to the fact that women have played a key role. Eighty percent of the borrowers are women. Professor Muhammad Yunus explains women's contribution to the success of the Grameen Bank:

> Women experience poverty and hunger much more intensively than men because they are traditionally the ones expected to look after the house and feed the children with virtually no money at all.
> It's women who suffer the greatest deprivation and have to make the greatest sacrifices. They are the ones who experience the most traumas when their children go hungry or fall ill. Give women like that a chance to fight hunger and poverty, and you'll find they're pluckier than their menfolk.

What he's saying is just as true of women in our country. Every Newfoundland government in living memory has promised to give top priority to local and small-scale development. Here's a model our government might look at. If this kind of a loan system were set in place for our province, we could begin to see long-term, small development taking place that could bring lasting results. People have a vested interest in making their communities work. And women's creativity and imagination would be one of the driving forces just as they are in Bangladesh.

Lest anyone think this scheme can only work in Third World countries, think again. It's a simple plan to imitate, and something like it has already been introduced in the city of Chicago for low-income women.

6 Family Matters

All too often, we have searched for family values and for the value of our families in the wrong places.
Robert Glossop, Vanier Institute,
in an address at Memorial University, January 25, 1994.

ALL IN THE FAMILY

At the beginning of 1987, it was announced that the Lieutenant Governor of Newfoundland and Labrador, the Honourable James McGrath, would be convening a committee to look into the state of the family in Newfoundland. It sounded like a laudable initiative and was the sort of thing we had come to expect from Mr. McGrath, a man known for pursuing goals with principle and passion. During his tenure in the House of Commons, he had won the respect of all parties.

When the announcement was made, there were no details about who was to be on the committee, what groups were to be represented, or what direction the committee would take on this complex and important subject. As I waited to hear more about it, I had some observations and suggestions to offer.

In proposing such a committee, the Lieutenant Governor was clearly interested in promoting the values we like to think are traditionally associated with family life: love, caring, mutual support, protection and all the rest. However, I could only hope that the committee would not take it for granted that by supporting all or only traditional nuclear families, they would automatically be reinforcing those values.

While those of us who have been lucky have found warmth and nurturing in our family lives, the sad fact is that for many others the family has been a place of torment. If one has had the good fortune to live in a family that operates on love and respect, it is easy to assume that most people share a similar experience.

A friend in the women's movement put me right about that. After we had known one another for some time, she finally told me that every time I used the word "family" in a positive way she wanted to object. For her, the term conjured up only the bitterest memories of fear, hostility, and violence. That conversation has since been reinforced many times by writers and dramatists and community counsellors.

It is hardly surprising if a person with negative experiences is less than enthusiastic about measures intended to strengthen the family. For many people, the family was far *too* strong—strong enough to trap them and hurt them and allow them no means of escape. Not so long ago, divorces could be obtained only through an order in parliament, and only on the grounds of adultery. Many people believed that making divorce difficult was a good thing because it "saved" marriages.

It was believed that if women were forced to stay in the home no matter what their problems, all would be well. Mothers gave their daughters the same sort of advice that Judge Bartlett used to dispense in Nova Scotia—that it was up to them to submit to their husbands: if they were abused or oppressed it was their own fault. Judge Bartlett has since been removed from the bench.

Many years ago I visited a young mother who had just returned from hospital after the birth of her second child. I found her in the kitchen, awkwardly perched on a stool, trying to wash the sink-full of pots and pans and dishes her husband had dirtied in her absence and left for her to clean.

The new baby was crying, the young mother was crying, and the older child was running about the house in a frenzy. The husband and father had gone off on a hunting trip with his friends. Some people regarded his behaviour as extreme, but nobody at the time regarded it as terribly unusual. Men didn't do housework. People tended to see it as something of a joke, illustrating what a macho "character" the man was.

Of course, men suffered too in unhappy family situations, but the main victims were women and children. The family was structured around the nearly absolute authority of men over women and parents over children, and in many families that authority took the form of vicious abuse, both mental and physical and sometimes incestuous as well.

In its desire to shore up the family unit, society took very little notice of the price it was forcing thousands of women and children to pay. Lawmakers, the police, courts, social workers, and clergy all co-operated in keeping victims in their homes.

There have been many changes for the better. Authorities now take family abuse much more seriously; transition houses provide support for battered women; it is easier to end an unworkable marriage. Attitudes have changed: women are developing a stronger sense of self-worth, and young people are more willing to accept the idea of equality of marriage partners.

Unfortunately, some people see these changes as a breakdown of the nuclear family and a threat to all the traditional values it is believed to represent. People who have worked for the changes, however, see them as supporting the same values. They do not want to break down the family, but to break down the rigidity, the inequality, and the injustice that the old family structure often embodied.

Nowadays, the values of caring, sharing and nurturing are finding expression in a wide variety of new family forms. The nuclear family makes up only a small percentage. So it is critical that the terms of reference of any committee examining the family be broad enough to include all family structures that are relevant today.

Single parenting is now an accepted option for some people. Other women and men choose to live together and perhaps have children, but to eschew legal marriage. Still others have chosen to share their lives in lesbian or gay relationships. Any of these forms can express the values of caring that we want to promote and should qualify for attention as bona fide families, represented in the deliberations of any committee on the family.

The key to making recommendations about the family surely lie in discerning the magical components of happy, enduring relationships, and determining what we can do as a society to shore up and strengthen those units that are built on love.

CHRISTMASTIME CONTRADICTIONS

Every Christmas, two organizations that I belong to, the Coalition of Citizens Against Pornography and the Voice of Women, place advertisements in the newspapers. Their purpose is to draw attention to a peculiar contradiction in our society that is particularly evident at Christmastime.

Picture an ordinary family gathered around the tree on Christmas morning. The children can hardly wait to see if Mom likes the present they have made for her. The parents have been hiding parcels in closets for weeks. The mantelpiece is decorated with dozens of cards bearing messages of good will. On the radio, carollers sing of peace and love and sharing.

The ten-year-old unwraps a present, and it's just what he wanted—Sgt. Slaughter, with Triple-Tracked Tank and Side-Mounted Guns! His little sister's wish has come true too: she got a blonde bombshell of a doll, with a body that would not be out of place in a *Playboy* centrefold, an unlimited consumer appetite, and a singleminded dedication to being a sex object. And their 14-year-old brother is delighted. He's just unwrapped the album all the kids have been talking about—the one with the scantily clad woman, all bruised black and blue, on the cover.

The contrast is so stark that it seems almost unbelievable. As someone once said, it's a damn funny way to celebrate the birthday of the Prince of Peace.

The parents who are spending their hard-earned money on these gifts that are diametrically opposed to the message of Christmas are, for the most part, gentle, kind people who only want happiness for their children. Many feel the contradiction but feel powerless to do anything about it. They're caught in the grip of a massive advertising machine and so are their kids.

The situation is worse in the United States where, according to an article in *MacLean's* magazine, at least twenty television programs aimed at children are directly controlled by toy companies. For hours every day children are bombarded with the most powerful and sophisticated thought control the world has ever seen. The main messages seem to be sexism, avaricious consumerism and violence.

Dr. Thomas Radecki, research director of the Illinois-based National Coalition on Television Violence has said, "There has never been a time when a nation's children have been subjected to such a massive promotion of sadistic and intensely violent material."

For the teenagers, the lessons are continued in song lyrics, magazines, videos and movies. Parents are subject to peer pressure too. Every year the Coalition Against Pornography gets calls from ordinary people telling of Christmas house parties where somebody brings out a really hot video that everyone must see.

I've heard from women who told me how degraded they felt at the time and how much they wanted to leave. They are confused about their reasons for staying and tell of the arguments with their husbands or partners on the way home. Sometimes the couple end up agreeing on their mutual discomfort and conclude that, although neither one wanted to stay, they didn't want to embarrass their hosts and were afraid that people would think them prudes. That shared understanding is not always the case. Many women are left hurt and disturbed because their husbands saw no reason for their distress.

The Christmastime contradictions are not just in toys or in entertainment. It is a sad fact that at this time of year transition houses for battered women experience an increase in emergency calls. For many women and children the Christmas season is a time of dread and foreboding. It's a time when all emotions are heightened, and when many men, the products of a society that condones sexism and violence, take out drunken frustrations on their wives and children.

It happens at every level of society: professional, working-class, educated, uneducated, young and old, rich and poor. Battering happens to one Canadian women out of eight, up from 1 in 10 a few years ago. The women who are being beaten need the help provided by transition houses, but many have to be turned away because there's no room. There is one bit of good news in this regard; in 1992, the St. John's Rotary raised $200,000 for the Iris Kirby Transition House. But it's time we attacked the root causes in any case.

Most of the public expressions of concern have come from women's groups and that's not good enough. Women aren't the problem; for the most part they are the victims. If 10 percent of men are the abusers then we need help from the remaining majority. Some men have been actively opposing pornography. In Halifax a men's group took on the campaign against war toys last year, giving out brochures and talking, particularly to other men, about the need to protect children from violence.

We need men's groups informing themselves about wife beating, about child abuse, about damaging images of women. We need men actively seeking solutions and applying their own peer pressure on their buddies who are the offenders.

We've got to work together on this so that the real Christmas messages can be enjoyed by everyone.

FAMILY VALUES

The speaker was Dr. Robert Glossop of the Vanier Institute in Ottawa, and his subject was family values. Not the sentimental ramblings of a George Bush or Dan Quayle—this was an address made in Canada for Canadians, built on our experience, on our societal ethics and present challenges. Dr. Glossop's audience at Memorial University was fascinated.

We've come to know and respect the work of the institute that bears the name of the late Governor-General, Major-General Georges Vanier. He and his wife, Pauline, won admiration during the early sixties for their demonstrated concern for the poor and the humble, for youth and for the family.

Their combined influence was eloquently displayed by their son, Jean, who is known worldwide with great affection for his work with the handicapped, for his belief that every human has special value. The institute grew out of that background and has held a special place of respect for thinkers and planners of social development.

We are saturated these days with messages that tell us that cutbacks must come from programs that aid human development. But that's not what Dr. Glossop is saying. He's talking about the need to reinforce and strengthen the family unit, of whatever composition. Many politicians, he said, are fond of piously stating that the family is the backbone of society. However, he prefers to turn it around: a decent society is the foundation of the family. Our social programs that support the family he regards as primary, a basic necessity for a reasonable society.

He argues against the notion of "privatizing" the family and leaving them on their own without the help and security nets offered by many different programs. He is disturbed that Canada has lost family allowances and also—without our knowledge even—has cut back on income tax provisions for children. For example, when families did their returns for Revenue Canada in 1994, they discovered that deductions for two children were all you got. Any more children would no longer be deductible.

These moves are detrimental to the family values that we espouse. We know that security and opportunity must be present for families to have hope, and that family breakup often occurs when the load of anxiety has become more than one can bear.

Dr. Glossop spoke of the pressures on today's families, noting that it now takes two incomes for most people to live at a decent level. And he described the nightmare of parents trying to beat the clock with a rush to the school or baby-sitter on the way to the office or other job, the rush home to prepare dinner, to wash the clothes, to make the cookies for the concert, to supervise the homework. He spoke of how we try to order our lives to have quality time with our children. We make appointments to be with them. He acknowledged that in saying those things he knew he was talking about the fortunate ones who have jobs.

But when these are the realities people face and we know that it's an unfair burden, then new ways must be found to strengthen the family unit, to make it possible for parents and children to have time together that is rewarding for both. We don't need fewer possibilities, as some would have it; we need more systems of support. Daycare is one such support. A shorter work week is another. And financial breaks in income tax and government policies that aid the development of children and parents would also help. It all makes good sense, but don't hold your breath while waiting for government to work these themes into their planning.

Indeed, there is evidence that things are going the other way. In 1995, the Liberal government backed away from earlier commitments to social programs, systematically destroying the safety net that Dr. Glossop says is so necessary to a decent family life.

TIME TO BE YOURSELF

I was talking one September day with a young friend of mine who had just returned to work after spending the summer being a full-time mother to her own children, as well as looking after the children of friends. I asked how she was and learned rather quickly that she was frazzled. It had been a long, hot summer.

She spoke of having the best husband in the world who was always willing to do everything for the kids and around the house. But it didn't matter how good he was; the burden still fell on her. If things were to be done she would have to organize it, and if they weren't done it was she who felt the load of guilt. She had some work of her own that she was hoping to produce but it never got off the ground. There were so many distractions. "You can't be creative yourself with small children," she said, "I'm so glad to be back at work. I've been going mad all summer."

This is a woman who thoroughly enjoys motherhood and takes her two girls everywhere. But she is used to having a part-time job where her writing and artistic skills come into play. She missed that during the holidays. It always sounds so easy in theory that a woman or a man should be able to organize parenting and still have time to themselves, but for most of us that just isn't so. Not without extra help.

We were able to laugh at what is women's familiar complaint. At least I was able to laugh—she was still recovering. But it did take me back to the time when our three were little. I can remember one occasion when I almost threw one of my dear children into my mother's arms as she came through the door. I had been up all night for several nights in a row trying to ease the baby's whooping cough. I couldn't take another bout of crying.

My mother brought me instant sanity. She laughed at me, which helped. I started to relax as she sang and cuddled her grandchild in her arms, and strength and reason started to come back. It only took a few minutes to feel better. That must have been one of the strengths of the extended family in the past: there was always another woman to take the sick child on her lap.

At a Christmas party one year, I was talking to a woman of my age who told me of her own feelings of entrapment when the children were small. She was wise enough at the time to write about those feelings and put it all down in a daily diary. Her grownup daughters now have a wonderful account of their own childhood—but just as important—they also have a deep understanding of their mother, her longings, her trials and tribulations.

We talked at length about how much it meant to have some free time to yourself, when you weren't at the beck and call of anyone. I was describing a system that used to operate in our house which I found enormously helpful. One day a month my husband would bring his work home and attempt to do it along with looking after the kids, the dog, the cat, the fish and the house. It was wonderful to leave the house early in the morning and forget about all the responsibilities at home, knowing that there was nothing to worry about. I could let my mind wander and do anything on a whim. I could go anywhere and return as late as I liked.

At first it took a long time to get used to not phoning in, but I knew if I did there would be some errand to run. If I did the errand the luxury of the day would be spoiled, and if I didn't do it I would be haunted by housewife's guilt. So I steeled myself to stay away from the phone.

Another trap that needed avoiding was that, as the magic day approached, there would be a dozen reasons to postpone it. We soon realized, however, that it would never happen unless we took it seriously. So nothing short of dire illness, flood or armed revolution was allowed to intervene. The event was sacred, and not to be tampered with.

The day was such a joy and filled with so many experiences that it was as good as a two-week holiday. I browsed through old book stores, sat motionless in art galleries, fed peanuts to squirrels (this was in Toronto) and walked miles in every direction. The beauty about being alone is that you have time to think and let your thoughts develop. Many of the world's problems were solved or at least wrestled with on those explorations as I pondered the meaning of life and how things could be...if only. And one of the "if onlys" that I would put at the top of the list is that if only we cared deeply enough about the nurturing of children, we would work harder at providing more choices to parents so that there would be less strain and more time for joy.

A medical specialist moving to St. John's provided me with an example of one type of choice. He delayed his appointment by six months so that he could take time out to be a full-time father. He and his wife take turns at round-the-clock parenting. That's the kind of flexibility we need to build into all workplaces so that this kind of thing could happen more often. There's a benefit for all family members but there's one for society too.

PARENTING

Among the many pleasant things about having all our grown children home together for a holiday is the way old memories get brought to the surface. Of course, not everybody remembers the same things—or wants to. Our three, if they get started on it, can produce a maddening collection of apparently indelible memories of childhood frustrations—the times they were refused ice cream, spending money or trips to the movies. The time we wouldn't stop the car to go to Fantasyland. They can give chapter and verse about being passed over while someone else got a special treat or whatever.

But ask them about those wonderful, unforgettable (to parents) moments at family reunions, science fairs or on summer holidays, not to mention trips across Canada by train and by car and you get frowns of puzzled concentration and maybe, "Well, I think I sort of remember that..."

We travelled by car, in the summer of 1972, from Vancouver to St.

John's. We drove hard, getting up almost with the dawn so that we could find a motel early and still have time for fun later in the day. Each spot had its own special treat. We went on the cable car across the Fraser River, swam in the hot springs in Banff, witnessed a rainbow filling the sky and listened to bluebirds on the prairies. We followed safely behind a thunderstorm in northern Ontario, watching for miles as it followed the Trans Canada highway just ahead of us, dropping bursts of torrential rainfall between thunderbolts and flashes of lightning.

We visited a dinosaur park in Calgary, ate in a French restaurant in old Montreal, watched the falls reversing in New Brunswick, had a meal of lobster on the shore of the Atlantic Ocean and boarded the ferry at Sydney, chock full of excitement. My eldest son does remember staying up all night to watch Port aux Basques appear through the mist in the early morning. And our second son remembers each animal and flower including the tiny marmot he found on the mountain at Banff, hiding behind the alpine flora. I'll give them that. But my daughter's deepest memory about that marvellous trip was that I "forced" them all to eat granola for breakfast.

My family in British Columbia had helped me prepare countless little bags of the most nutritious granola, full of delicious nuts and fruits and grains, so that we could get away smartly in the morning without stopping for breakfast. I'm a great believer in the connection between full stomachs and jolly dispositions, so yes, I did push granola. I know you're not supposed to force children about food, but it's true. I did it and I may never be forgiven.

Another memory that all three seem to possess is the "forced" exercise that their father imposed on them, and their deep embarrassment at standing on the side of the Trans Canada while he made sounds like a Sergeant-Major: "Up, down, up down!" He insisted that we all do this together. He believed that a bit of vigorous activity once in a while would cut down on the crabby lethargy that goes with long car trips. He may have been right, but he may never be forgiven either.

After listening for a while to these biased accounts, my husband and I go over our own tender memories when the "children" are not around.

We sometimes laugh about our first year of marriage. As everybody knows, so many adjustments and new experiences take place. I know it was my mother and her many cups of tea that prevented us from heading for the divorce court after our bitter experience at trying to wallpaper a ceiling for the first and last time. Why were we wallpapering a ceiling? Don't ask. It seemed the thing to do at the time.

Still, I resent being the one who held the broom that held the wallpaper to the ceiling and therefore the one who caught the full impact of being swathed in wet, freshly pasted paper that repeatedly hurtled down and wound itself around me. Once might be accidental. Even amusing. But three times?

And I only once made the mistake of thinking it was funny to throw a bucket of snow at a naked man having a shower. I have never done it again.

It was by sheer accident that we did at least one thing that turned out to be exactly right. We were both at university as mature students the year our first child was born. He arrived at the beginning of the reading week preceding exams, so new parents and new baby had to get to know each other in the midst of books, notes and papers.

As pressures on campus were equal, it followed that pressures at home would have to be too. One night I would be on full maternal duty, checking every few minutes to make sure the baby was covered, breathing, dry, fed, whatever. The next night it was his father's turn while I slept the sleep of the just—and just barely awake when the baby was brought to me to feed. He was changed, burped, walked and sung to while I heard none of it.

My husband became so competent with this little creature that my own mother used to politely suggest that I should leave the baby's bath until all hands were present because his dad was so good at it. I was quick to agree because, as we all know, bathing your first child is a very big production, and my hands never seemed to offer the same security.

After exams were over and our newborn was awarded an honourary diploma in Social Work, we found that I could get summer employment so father took over the home. Some pretty ridiculous scenes came out of that one. He used to wear a rather hideous butcher's apron over a pair of shorts while doing the housework. Once, he answered the door with a mop in one hand and the baby tucked under his arm, his hairy chest and legs displayed above and below what appeared to be his only garment. He said it was the first time he ever saw a pair of Jehovah's Witnesses speechless.

I know it used to upset the other husbands on the block. They would tell him rather strongly that they didn't want to hear another word about the tough day he had put in. They considered him a bit of a bore at neighbourhood parties when he would insist that they had no idea what went into running a home. The women thought he was wonderful, of course. One friend used to tell me that she repeatedly invited him over for coffee when she caught him running to the garbage can or putting clothes on the line, just so she could hear all the common housewife's complaints delivered in a masculine growl: he hadn't a thing in the house for supper, the diapers had boiled over (we used to wash them in those days). He had just learned that his brother's family would be visiting for the weekend, and that meant he had to clean the guest room. And what on earth would he feed them? The house was a mess—how can one small glass of orange juice cover a whole kitchen?

He told his male friends that he had thought housework was a simple case of efficient organization—but that he hadn't known about the phone always ringing, or how you feel after a night of walking a sick child, or why babies take so long to eat, or that a doctor's appointment can screw up your whole day.

I, on the other hand, would tell the wives on the block that when I got home at 5:30 I was beat. I wanted to play with my son, but I wanted him clean and fed, so that we could simply hug and have fun together. I didn't particularly want to hear about the cat breaking the basement window or the leak in the bathroom. I had a lot to talk about too and it seemed more important to tell about the injustices that happened that day at city social services.

And no, thank you, I wasn't terribly keen to go to a movie. I thought it would be really nice to just sit around, with my feet up, and read a bit.

It was great. For both of us. And for our son. Putting yourself in somebody else's shoes is a pretty good way to find out where they pinch.

THE GREAT ESCAPE

We were hurrying along Kenmount Road just before store closing time, intent on picking up those essential pieces of hardware that would ensure a working weekend. Doors would once more swing free on their hinges, windows would open and close without threatening hernia. There's a lot to be said for weekends of putting domestic things right.

Suddenly my husband applied the brakes, bringing the car to a full and startling stop. In front of us, in the midst of all that traffic, was the most stately of mother ducks with a brood of eleven tiny ducklings. Frightened, in desperation, the mother duck threaded her way through the impossible traffic with her babies after her and turned into a gas station parking lot. We pulled in too, and for the next half hour followed behind and around the brood trying to help others in the panic to keep them safe from being trampled or run over.

Right from the beginning there was one young man in a navy blue sweater who knew best what was happening and understood what we must do. He told us that the mother duck knew exactly where she was going. If we could all stay out of her way, she would be able to reach O'Leary's Brook where it appears from underground in the southeast corner of the Avalon Mall parking lot, just before it goes under Thorburn road. He was sure that was where she wanted to go. But it was a long way from where they were.

He figured that the brood had got caught in the current upstream, which suddenly becomes very strong just before the brook goes underground on the other side of the mall. He conjectured that the mother duck had probably rescued them from the current, and was now trying to walk her way through the crowded mall parking lot to get to the place where the river picks up again.

The hazards were monumental. It was the usual Friday night mall scene, with the little bit extra that goes with the beginning of a holiday weekend: trying enough for human beings, but overwhelming for a family of ducks. The lot was full of parked cars, moving cars, and people walking purposefully in all directions.

The ducks never stopped. The mother held her head high the whole time, looking left and right and changing direction in an instant if something threatening appeared, keeping up a constant low quacking.

The babies scuttled along in single file behind their mother, their little legs a blur of movement, peeping constantly like a roomful of tiny video games. They crossed the entrance road, cars slowing and stopping to let them pass, and reached the yellow curb. The mother hopped up and set off across the grass divider—but without her brood. The ducklings were milling in confusion at the foot of this towering cliff that had suddenly appeared in their path. Helpful people tried to herd them along to a break in the curb, but suddenly one little individualist shot off in the opposite direction, cheeping wildly, and others went with him. After a good deal of running about by ducks and people, the ducks were reunited on the other side of the barrier, and Mother Duck set them off across the crowded parking lot.

Children who came upon the scene were overjoyed and let out appreciative screams, calling "Come here, come here," with outstretched arms. It was hard to look at the ducklings without wanting to cuddle them. But of course it had the opposite effect, causing the babies to run more frantically and the mother to veer and turn, now this way and now that way, and now in the opposite direction from where she wanted to go.

Shoppers would round a corner and let out a gasp of astonished delight to see twelve ducks disappearing under their car. But delight quickly turned to concern, and the crowd of protectors grew.

All the erratic turning brought the ducks closer to the stream, but also to the stores where there were more people and more cars. At one point, the frantic mother took to her wings. She flew in a panic just over the cars and the people, staying close to the brood but above the confusion. She circled around and around until she could chance again to settle for a minute or two on the sidewalk with her babies. It was pathetic to watch her desperate attempts to protect them in the face of so many hazards.

The man-in-the-navy-blue-sweater proved to be the man of the hour. He shouted directions at all of us to stem the tide of traffic. "Don't get too close to the birds! They're heading for the stream. Somebody get out front to stop the cars. Not too close!" He finally got us organized into a large, loose circle around the birds, moving with them through the parked cars, stopping traffic and restraining over-enthusiastic children. Finally the little family began to make steady progress toward their goal.

And the moment came when that dear, determined mother duck led her brood as fast or faster than ever, across the lane where traffic usually flows in from Thorburn road, down over the hill, and into the water, sailing safely away in the direction of the Health Sciences Centre.

There were tears and laughter and applause as onlookers experienced relief and joy. We knew there would be other perils, but they had survived this one. And we all went home with happy memories of tiny little feathered creatures obediently following their brave mother to safety after enduring unimaginable terrors.

When you think about it, with all the time that was spent running backwards and forwards through the automotive jungle in the Avalon Mall parking lot on such tiny legs, it would be comparable to human beings running in terror with their young from St. John's to Holyrood or someplace, with the youngsters shouting at the top of their voices all the way. Amazing.

And the navy-blue-sweater man, when some of us thanked him for taking charge, gave only a taciturn comment, though he smiled proudly. As we said goodbye and went back to our cars, he said "I sure love wildlife." It showed, man, it showed.

So the doors still squeak and the windows still stick, but what the heck. It was worth it.

7 Eternal Vigilance

As women lead, they are changing leadership; as they organize, they are changing organization... When women lead and articulate their purposes, it seems to me that they work together not only as individuals but with a sense of community and networking in a healthy way... Women have fresh and imaginative skills of dialogue and are setting a more open, flexible and compassionate style of leadership.

Mary Robinson, President of Ireland,
quoted in the Newsletter of the
Women's Environment and Development Organization

WOMEN WINNING THE BATTLE OF LANGUAGE

Some years ago, the federal government announced plans for a brand new building to house the National Museum of Man. The museum had become one of the largest in the world and had long outgrown the building it had occupied since 1911.

The plan came to the attention of women's groups and we asked, through the National Action Committee on the Status of Women, that when the museum reopened it would do so under a different name—a name that would give equal recognition to the historical and cultural contributions of women as well as men.

Well, of course, the catcalls started. "There they go again making a fuss about nothing. What do women want anyway?" And the jokes started: "I suppose they'll want to change Pullman sleeping cars to Pullperson." And, "Will Deadman's Pond have to be Dead Peoples's Pond?" And, "Who's going to come around to the children at bedtime? The sandperson?"

Purists told us to stop tampering with the beauties of the English language. We were told that there was no other name that could adequately and properly describe the contents of the museum and that, in any case, the word "man" included woman.

We were told that if we continued in our foolish ways it might require an expensive nationwide campaign to find an appropriate title, and we were cautioned to stop being so sensitive or we would lose public respect.

The response was all too familiar. Those of us who had been around for a while in the women's movement were used to similar angry resistance every time we suggested a change in customary ways of using language.

Remember the fuss about "Ms.?" What a carry-on there was when that idea was first broached! You can't pronounce it. It looks funny. It sounds like something out of *Gone With the Wind*. It will never catch on. It's not proper etiquette. It did sound awkward at first, even to the people promoting it, but we were beginning to recognize the important connection between language and social attitudes. Before Ms, a woman's value was measured by whether or not she had a man.

The young male, as soon as he reached a certain age, became a Mister. His status as a man was assured and independent of other relationships. The woman who went beyond girlhood as a Miss, on the other hand, was always regarded as deficient in some way, and was subjected to either sympathy or scorn.

Today, in spite of all the resistance, Ms. is firmly established. The news media, governments, business and industry all use it as a matter of routine. Many official forms allow women to choose among three titles. Society has acknowledged an important principle: that women can be seen as individuals rather than as appendages of men.

While the battle over Ms. was going on, feminists were also challenging other usages, such as the custom of referring to "the chairman" when a woman was in the chair or the whole human race as "mankind."

Often it is hard for people to see the point of the argument. Most of us are not used to analyzing the way we say things. If the word "man" is commonly used to refer to the whole human race, then that is what we use without considering the implications. However, as writer Elaine Morgan has pointed out:

> If you write a book about Man or conceived a theory about Man you cannot avoid using the word. You cannot avoid using the pronoun as a substitute for the word, and you will use the pronoun "he" as a simple matter of linguistic convenience. But before you are halfway through the first chapter a mental image of this creature begins to form in your mind. It will be a male image and he will be

the hero of the story; everything and everyone else in the story will relate to him...

For years, scientists and historians have been protesting that there is nothing wrong with customary usage. Like the planners of the new museum, they thought we were being paranoid. "Of course when we say Man, we include women," they would say. Sometimes they would add the patronizing old joke, "Everybody knows that *man* embraces *woman*!"

But a close examination of what was being written tells a different story. Writer Dale Spender provides some fairly typical examples, like the world-famous psychiatrist who defined Man's vital interests as "life, food, access to females, etc." or the anthropologist who wrote of Man that "his back aches, he ruptures easily, his women have difficulties in childbirth." Presumably these eminent scholars believed that they were using the word Man to refer to the whole species. It seems incredible that they apparently did not notice how they had relegated half the human race to an inferior status.

The women's movement has learned that, in spite of what Shakespeare said about roses, it *does* matter what we call things. It especially matters what we call people. A word like chairman applied indiscriminately to males and females makes a statement about the relative importance and value of women and men. We are asking for different statements.

And we are having some success. The language is changing. Public speakers, official documents, and the media all now routinely refer to "men and women" where once they would have referred only to men; it's common practice now to read "he or she" and "his or her" where once they would have insisted on only the masculine pronoun. They tend to put the masculine form first all the time, but never mind, progress is being made all the same.

In fact, it is now the old-fashioned and sexist terms that are startling when we come upon them. For example, it was a shock when, in an announcement of the appointment of a woman as company manager, the woman was identified by her husband's two names. Or when a well-known provincial politician referred to the "city fathers of St. John's" in a letter to the editor, in spite of the fact that the deputy mayor and another councillor were women. Wouldn't you think he'd have noticed?

The museum? It was reopened as the National Museum of Civilization. One small step for humankind.

GANGING UP AGAINST WOMEN

On February 12, 1981, 1300 hundred women converged on the West Block on Parliament Hill for a most unusual meeting. Long-term plans for a conference to be held on "Women and the Constitution" scheduled for around that time had been arbitrarily postponed by the Liberal government. We were moving into a pre-election period and the government didn't want women raising embarrassing questions about being left out of the Constitution.

When the original conference was called off, alarm bells rang across the nation. The freshly appointed President of the first Canadian Advisory Council on the Status of Women, Doris Anderson, resigned in protest. So did many of her colleagues.

All across Canada, women dropped whatever they were doing to hold emergency meetings. Within a few days a country-wide consensus was reached: we would hold the conference anyway, whether the government wanted it or not.

Never mind that there was no funding to send delegates. Never mind that Ottawa hotels were full, and plane tickets hard to come by. Almost overnight, money was raised until every province had enough to send delegates to speak up for the rest of us. Women in Ottawa did their best to provide billeting. Women from east, west, and north brought their sleeping bags and bunked down on chesterfields and floors. Hotel rooms doubled their occupancy.

It was a critical time. Prime Minister Trudeau had repatriated the Constitution and added the Charter of Rights and Freedoms to it. Nobody quite knew what the implications were. Parliamentarians and concerned citizens were analyzing what it would mean for the country.

The original conference was planned to allow women discussion and debate on what the Charter held in store for them. Women's groups had already made presentations to the Special Committee on the Constitution and as a result some improvements had been made. But women still weren't happy with the latest proposals. The best legal minds in the feminist community could find no assurance that women's rights would be adequately protected.

At the ad hoc meeting, women representing all three parties agreed that a special passage must be added to the Charter guaranteeing women's equality. Following the meeting, delegates went back to their homes and organized a relentless campaign of consciousness-raising and lobbying. An all-party committee in Ottawa spent the time lobbying every member on the Hill. Women were contacted. Telegrams sent. MPs and Premiers visited. Newspapers and media alerted. Confrontations took place between women and local politicians who didn't want to be counted.

Finally it worked. Section 28 was added to the Charter. The troublesome equality clause that caused such furore reads:

Notwithstanding anything in this Charter, the rights and freedoms referred to in it are guaranteed equally to male and female persons.

In April, 1981, the House of Commons unanimously passed this new clause.

There was jubilation across the land. We had secured for Canadian women the same rights and freedoms that would be afforded to men. Or so we thought. Experienced feminists weren't so sure. They knew that eternal vigilance is the price of equality as well as democracy and they kept their eye on what was transpiring day by day and became uneasy.

The First Ministers continued their examination of the proposed constitutional package, and in November, after three days of negotiations, worked out something called an "override" that would apply to *certain sections* of the Charter's promised rights and freedoms. It meant that either the federal government or a provincial government could ignore the provisions of that particular designated section anytime it wished, under a five-year renewal plan.

For weeks, women's groups in every province demanded to know from their local premier whether our hard-won Section 28 was subject to the override. We were told a lot of things. That we were being silly. That we were paranoid. That we had no trust. That we had everything we wanted. And that of course we were protected.

We compared notes across the country and didn't like what we were hearing. Through the smoke of denial it became clear to us that the old boys club of First Ministers had done something women wouldn't like and had agreed that no one would spill the beans.

Women were pretty sure we were being lied to.
Eventually one of the premiers confessed. He told the truth to a leading woman in his party. She immediately contacted women across Canada and all hell broke loose. We *had* been lied to, and every party was guilty. Section 28, guaranteeing women's rights equal to men's, had been made subject to the override!

That really united Canadian women. Differences were thrust aside, and intense lobbying efforts mounted again with redoubled vigour. From all walks of life, women demanded of every premier that the override clause be lifted from Section 28. After a sustained effort, success was finally ours and remains so. Bet that story isn't in the history books.

The Canadian Advisory Council on the Status of Women issued a guidebook, authored by Penny Kome, called *Play From Strength* that built upon women's constitutional struggle. Kome concludes:

> ...women tend to be pulled into political action for a variety of reasons. We hope that once you have become politicized, you will want to remain active. Women discovered a new solidarity and a profound political strength during the 1981 constitutional lobby. That strength must be exercised regularly, or it will atrophy.

In 1995, the Chrétien Liberal government took away our Canadian Advisory Council on the Status of Women.

HOME ECONOMICS

At the 1994 Women's International Conference on Sustainable Development in Vancouver, one of the presenters posed the question, "Why do men in power talk about the economy as though there is only one kind?" "The economy" is presented as a fixed entity to which the unwashed multitudes are expected to give respect and obeisance. Politicians, bureaucrats and economists suggest that they understand the beast in a way that the rest of us could never manage to do.

Well, that way of thinking got short shrift from the female activists at this Vancouver conference. "You can design the economy to achieve your goals," the women said, and went on from there to talk about a feminist vision of economics.

In one group I was in we were trying to find better words to describe the sentiments we shared. A woman from Peru said, "You keep using the word "community", Dorothy, but I prefer the word "home." We thought about that, and liked the concept that the word suggested, because not only does "home" denote those you love—family and friends—it also includes the place, the town, the village, the outport and the country that you identify with. It also signifies that the planet is our shared home. And it follows that we have to protect all of them with the same determination and zeal that we would our domestic home.

It didn't take long in our workshop to find the phrase that seemed to wrap up the direction we wanted to move in, and from then on we talked feminist-talk about the need for "Home Economics." We liked the twist of the phrase and the connection it made with women's work and the world's needs. And then we started analyzing the foolishness of present day economics.

Gloria Steinem has described New Zealand economist Marilyn Waring as one who "demystifies both national and international economics... she not only puts human beings and human values into economics, but also vice versa." Those are the kind of economics that this women's conference endorsed one hundred percent.

Waring took Toronto and Ottawa audiences by storm a few years ago when she was on a speaking and book promotion tour on her way to Brazil to the United Nations Conference on Sustainable Development. She just makes so much sense that audiences—particularly, but not only, women—feel immediately connected with her analysis. For one thing she's big on the fact that women's work is unaccounted for in national economic indicators, and this is the kind of thing we were talking about.

On the cover of Waring's book, *If Women Counted*, is a quote from economist John Kenneth Galbraith:

> I've often commented on the way the work of women is excluded from our national accounting and overlooked in economics in general. And, alas, I've done very little about it. Now this splendid work goes far to fill this appalling gap. No concerned women (or man) can ignore it.

Waring asks why it is that water in a pipe has economic value but that water being carried daily in long distances on the heads of women does not.

She queries why it is that trees have an economic value when they are chopped down and cut up into lumber but have no value when they are left standing, providing us with oxygen to breathe?

She talks about the idiocy that environmental resources that we value are excluded from measure in the economy, but the destruction of these resources and the costs of cleaning up the mess are labelled as indicators of growth. For example, The Exxon Valdez oil spill in Alaska actually raised the local Gross Domestic Product.

In Feminist Home Economics, our workshop agreed, parks and beaches and trees would be recognized as essential to human well-being and of estimable value. We knew that women's anger at environmental destruction must be channelled to effect change.

Waring puts it this way:

> We must remember that true freedom is a world without fear. And if there is confusion about who will achieve that, then we must each of us walk to a clear pool of water. Look at the water. It has value. Now look into the water. The woman we see there counts for something. She can help to change the world.

Terri Nash and Studio D of the National Film Board produced a film about Marilyn Waring, called *Who's Counting*? After leaving politics, Waring went back to University to work out a new system of economics that more closely represents the true wealth of a nation, including environmental concerns and women's work.

ONCE UPON A TIME

There are parts of this story that some people may find difficult to believe. But it is a true story, nevertheless.

Once upon a time there was a woman named Emily Ferguson who was born in Cookstown, Ontario, in 1868. Her father was a wealthy man, as were her grandfather and all her uncles. Among them they controlled great land holdings and several newspapers. Members of the family sat as judges on provincial courts and on the Supreme Court of Canada.

Emily's brothers were encouraged at an early age to go into law, but Emily, like other young women of her day, was protected from the corrupting knowledge of things legal, political and economic. Like her mother before her, she was encouraged to maintain a purity of mind. She was sent to an expensive private school where religious instruction ensured that only the noblest of thoughts would be presented to the vulnerable young women students. They were taught decorum and deportment, and, perhaps most of all, obedience to a system designed by the men who were in control of it—that is, her grandfather and father and uncles and brothers, and their colleagues and friends.

Pretty dresses the young women had by the score. Wonderful hats with roses and ribbons were theirs for the asking. They only knew what was beautiful and pleasant, like coming-out parties and dancing with handsome, eligible young men who came from equally important families, and who one day would take control of things from their fathers, just as good men have forever been taught to do.

Emily and her sisters, of course, knew nothing of the less attractive side of the rapidly growing industrial city where they lived. They were not told of the sweatshops on Spadina Avenue, where less fortunate women and their children worked twelve and fourteen hours a day in dangerous and often unbearable conditions for less money than Emily put on the collection plate on Sunday morning. They were certainly never allowed to wander into the sordid slums where these women and their families lived.

At the age of 19, Emily married Arthur Murphy, an Anglican minister of 30. Nothing wrong with that—except that he seems to have been the wrong sort of Anglican minister. Emily's days of innocence were numbered.

For ten years she worked alongside her husband in small communities in Ontario, where she was surprised to see a society totally different from her own. The couple moved to England for a time on the invitation of the Mission Society and during their stay the veils of affluence were lifted completely. Emily saw, firsthand, the hidden side of the most advanced industrial nation in the world. She was shocked by the fetid slums and the crippling poverty that was everywhere.

She began to harbour the sort of impure thoughts that her family had tried so hard to protect her from. She questioned why people had to live in such squalid conditions, and—oh, the iniquity of a corrupted female mind—even made suggestions as to how life could be improved for them. Had she married a wealthy lawyer or respected judge, befitting her station in life, we may be sure he would have protected her from such wicked ideas.

But worse was yet to come. Under the pen name of Janey Canuck she began to publish her dangerous thoughts in books. Back in Canada, in an isolated village in northern Manitoba, she pressured officialdom into building a hospital. She was impressed with the lifestyle of a religious community of Doukhobors. She admired their method of sharing resources and the fact that men and women contributed equally to decision making. As is so often the case, one impure thought led to another, and before long Emily Murphy set out to liberate women. She believed that if women could get the vote and equality with men they could use their experiences to change society so that all people would share in the riches of a nation.

The family moved to Edmonton in 1908 when Emily was 40. She worked with suffragists like Nellie McClung to demand the vote for women. She worked to overturn the property laws of Alberta that decreed that all property in a marriage belonged to the husband. She pushed and lobbied to establish agencies to protect children. She worked for the rights of those most vulnerable: patients in mental institutions, prisoners, the young, the elderly. She produced exposé after exposé on corruption and useless administrations, and encouraged other women to do the same.

She organized the first "Federated Women's Institute" and became its president. Her contribution to social reform was recognized, and in 1916 she was made the first woman magistrate in the British Empire. It was beginning to seem as though Emily's thoughts weren't so impure after all.

But on her first day on the bench, Judge Murphy was challenged by a defence lawyer who claimed she had no right to be holding court. He said she was not a "person" and referred to British Common Law which held that "Women are persons in matters of pains and penalties but are not persons in matters of rights and privileges." And the defence lawyer was right. Women were not defined legally as persons.

Imagine the sort of thoughts that crossed Emily's mind that day! Thus began a battle to change the interpretation of federal law. Women's organizations rallied round. They pinpointed the Senate as a place to prove that women were persons and demanded that an appointment be given to Emily Murphy. But three prime ministers, one after the other, turned down their pleas. Borden, Meighan and even MacKenzie King (in spite of his mother fixation and his fondness for the "working girls" of Rideau Street) led the nation in denying women the legal status to be persons. The women took their case to the Supreme Court of Canada, and there five male judges agreed with the prime ministers. Of course, women were not persons.

What the judges' mothers, wives, daughters and sisters thought about their decision is not recorded.

Undaunted, Emily and four other suffragists—Nellie McClung, Irene Parlby, Henrietta Edwards and Louise McKinney—took the case to the highest court, the Privy Council of England. And so it was that Canadian women finally won their right to be persons. Lord Sankey, speaking for the Privy Council, stated that "The exclusion of women from all public offices is a relic of days more barbarous than ours."

On October 18, 1929, 13 years after her appointment to the bench, Judge Emily Murphy, aged 61, became a person at last. And, thanks to her and her stalwart sisters, so did all the women of Canada.

BUT FOR THE GRACE OF GOD

I would not want to be misconstrued. I do not condone biting policemen. And you can read that either way—biting *of* or *by* policemen. In fact, I don't approve of anybody biting anybody else, except maybe by mutual consent. All the same, there was something in a newspaper item I read a while ago that struck a chord with me.

It was one of those short pieces that are included for curiosity value, and it told of a woman being sent to jail for thirty days. It appears that she was stopped by a policeman for speeding. As the judge put it, "She didn't accept the ticket gracefully." Instead, "She walked into the middle of the street, saying she was going to kill herself." As the constable grasped her arms, she "bit his thumb to the bone...when he tried to handcuff her, she bit his left ring finger to the bone."

At first glance we are inclined to think it is a jolly good thing that she was put away. I mean, no normal woman would behave like that, would she?

Well, it appears that this woman is a single mother of four. She holds two part-time nursing jobs, and also sells real estate on the side. Once I had read that, my imagination began to fill in the details. I wondered: why was she speeding? Was she rushing off to pick up a child at a hockey practice or ballet lesson? Had the babysitter called in sick at the last minute? Was the plumbing blocked up back at home? Had she received a note from her oldest son's teacher asking her to drop in for a chat? Were health-care cutbacks threatening one or both of her part-time nursing jobs, and was the recession making it impossible to sell houses? I'll bet it was raining.

Now, I agree that she shouldn't have been driving so fast. And deciding to run into traffic to kill herself was not a great idea. And she certainly shouldn't have bitten the policeman. At least not to the bone. But I'm inclined to think that thirty days in jail are not going to do much to solve her problems.

The story sent my mind back more than thirty years. It was two days before my wedding. The week had seen my family's house getting fuller and fuller as the clan gathered for the big event. Wendy, my four-year-old niece and flower-girl-to-be, was playing in the basement and, when she came upon the washing machine, she naturally pulled all the levers and pushed all the buttons.

This was a strange old machine of a type I have never seen before or since. It worked on the boa constrictor principle. It didn't spin the water out of the clothes; it squeezed them by pumping water in and around the rubber lining of the tub. Of course it was essential that the lid be kept locked down or the lining would blow up through the opening like a huge grey balloon and finally explode, sending gallons of water cascading over the floor.

The lid wasn't locked down when Wendy pushed the levers, and she was pretty impressed with the result. So were the rest of us. With a wedding in the offing and a houseful of people, including a lot of little kids, a washing machine was of paramount importance.

My brother, who could fix anything, announced that he would install a new lining if somebody could locate one. Phone calls were made, and finally the only firm that carried this strange apparatus was found, away downtown in the industrial section of Vancouver. The parts department was about to close, but the bride-to-be cheerfully allowed that she would happily be the one to bring home the lining. And she would do this as the store opened at 8 a.m. the next morning. In an equally generous gesture, she would take along little Wendy and Wendy's equally frolicsome brother, Dougie, and treat them to breakfast at some exciting cafe so that other family members could get on with all the things that have to be done before a wedding.

We set off at 7:30 a.m., weaving our way between massive trucks down to the industrial section. I put a leash on Wendy and Doug, sallied up to the parts counter and waited cheerfully to ask for the new lining. The man at the counter, just as cheerfully, said that we had come to the wrong place. The only warehouse in Christendom that sold such a peculiar thing was located in an equally busy industrial section in New Westminster, almost an hour away.

By now all commerce was on the road. Roaring trucks moved materials from one end of the universe to another. Buses loaded with workers stopped every thirty feet. Cars were bumper to bumper. Horns were honking; fists were shaking.

Inside our car, the scene was quickly deteriorating. I was desperately re-arranging the day's schedule in my mind: essential shopping, buying presents for the attendants, meeting a friend at the airport, and the last-minute rehearsal.

Sweet little niece and nephew wanted the breakfast they had been promised, and upon being told that they would have to wait until after we got through the traffic, they began to fill the time by tormenting one another. Voices were raised and tears were shed.

We stopped at an intersection on Main Street where six or more lanes of traffic went in all directions, with the bride-to-be threatening her flower-girl-to-be with physical damage if she didn't leave her brother alone. The car on the right moved forward, and we did the same. Only he turned right while we went straight ahead through a red light and a stream of onrushing traffic.

The policeman on the other side of the intersection wearily waved me over to the curb and launched into a bored-sounding lecture as he began to write out a ticket. Behind me, Wendy and Doug howled in unison. I did the only thing that seemed reasonable at the time. I burst into tears. "But I'm getting married tomorrow," I blubbered. The cop's world-weary expression didn't change. "Congratulations," he said, and passed me the ticket.

For a second or two, his hand was right in front of my face. It is only by luck and Providence that it did not occur to me to bite him. I certainly thought of a lot of other things I might do to him. Only now, after reading that news report, do I realize what a close call we both had.

I feel sorry for the policeman who was bitten, to be sure. But mostly I feel sorry for that stressed-out single mother. I hope the thirty days gives her a bit of peace and quiet, but I don't suppose it will. The babysitter will be phoning her in prison to tell her that the dog got loose and was taken away to the pound and that the youngest has a rash that looks like measles. Rather than 30 days in prison, what she really needs is ten days at Disneyland with her kids, a reliable nanny, and a comfortable bed.

8 As the Stomach Turns

This material is exploitative of women—they are portrayed as passive victims who derive limitless pleasure from inflicted pain, and from subjugation to acts of violence, humilation and degradation. Women are depicted as sexual objects whose only redeeming features are their genital and erotic zones which are prominently displayed in minute detail.
Pornography and Prostitution in Canada,
Volume 1, p. 103

In 1983 we marched down Water street in St. John's to alert public attention to the fact that Pay Television intended to bring in Playboy movies and we asked—unsuccessfully—our watchdog, the Canadian Radio-television and Telecommunications Commission (CRTC) to stop it. Well, as they say, the rest is history.

THE DEBATE IS FAR FROM OVER

For quite a while after the federal government gave first reading to its 1987 pornography bill, I could find plenty of reasons not to write about it. I found it to be a difficult, tangled, unpleasant subject and, to be honest, I was thoroughly sick of it.

But it wouldn't go away. The commentaries kept piling up, and when Parliament reconvened in the fall, it would be back in the headlines again. I told myself I couldn't avoid it any longer.

It had been distressing to see and hear all the attacks on the bill in newspapers and magazines and on radio and television, especially when many of the commentators were people I knew and respected, and some were close friends.

Not that close friends can't disagree. It wouldn't be much of a friendship if you couldn't. What distressed me was that, with all the rhetoric and passionate argument, it was no longer very clear just what we were disagreeing about.

There were many times when the debate, if that is what it can be called, seemed like a manifestation of the silly season.

A political colleague of mine, whom I respected, denounced the bill in the House of Commons as expressing a "Victorian" mentality. I thought of the ugly, degrading material that had come to the attention of our Coalition Against Pornography. I found it a bit much to compare the pornography of today with a time when the sight of women's ankles was supposed to drive men into a frenzy of lust.

It was disturbing to see the serious concerns of the public being subjected to petty ridicule. To suggest that the bill would make it necessary for statues to wear fig leaves may have been good for a laugh, but it distorted the intent of the bill and did nothing to further rational discussion.

Three main positions were emerging in the debate over pornography. These positions remain much the same now. On the one side are people—and I am one of them—who believe that women and children are harmed by an industry that promotes their pain and humiliation. We believe that an industry so potentially harmful should be subject to control as other harmful products are controlled; we contend that this can be done without loss to legitimate artists.

At the other extreme are those who believe the greatest societal harm comes from censorship—any kind of censorship—and that to limit anyone's freedom of expression, no matter how brutal or repugnant we may find it, is to endanger everyone's liberty.

In between, there are people who accept the idea that some control is probably necessary but who fear that laws designed to limit the pornography industry may be used to threaten the freedom of expression of legitimate artists, and they are troubled by having to decide which of their concerns is paramount.

All three positions are held by reasonable, intelligent people, and all can be supported by serious, carefully considered arguments. That is why it is so patently unfair to see the debate reduced to ridicule, distortion, and name calling.

The media must bear a large part of the blame. While pretending to encourage a serious critique of the bill, they concentrated their interviews almost exclusively on people who take an anti-censorship position. It was particularly notable that they ignored the largest citizens' group in Canada that had been opposing pornography for years. Rose Potvin, president of the Coalition of Citizens Against Media Pornography, was never asked for her opinion.

Her organization has coordinated the work of provincial anti-porn groups across Canada. It has compiled statistics, analyzed research and accumulated a massive amount of knowledge and argument on the subject. If there had been an honest portrayal of public opinion, Potvin's contribution would have been vital. Yet with all the flurry of editorials and interviews on radio and television, in magazines and newspapers, only Peter Gzowski asked for her participation.

Rational debate was not what the media was after. We were subjected to a one-sided, media-biased campaign. Among the dozens who were interviewed to attack the bill, I think that many were not entirely honest—or perhaps not entirely clear in their own minds—about which position they were defending. They objected to this phrase or that, ridiculed a word here and there, and left the implication that faulty or inept wording forced them to render the whole bill invalid. If it were only a faulty section, why not point it out and suggest improvements? That's the normal procedure for refining any bill before parliament.

On the other hand, if you are opposed to any kind of censorship, why not say that and give up quibbling over wording? Or, if you would really like to control hard-core pornography but feel that it is impossible to create a law that will do it without endangering other freedoms, why not say so, instead of taking refuge in criticizing the wording? These are both defensible positions. I don't happen to agree with them, but I think I understand them and I'm willing to put up my own arguments against them.

I think that one of the reasons the debate didn't develop along these themes was that critics of the bill were well aware that the chief components for control—making it illegal to own or distribute child pornography and material that condones sexual violence—had widespread support.

It's a lot more comfortable to pick holes in some parts of a bill and then insist that the whole thing must be dropped. Easier, but not exactly honest.

Of course, there is always another category of critic whose members won't identify themselves. They are the ones who enjoy or profit from pornography, but are not about to say so. They are, however, certainly to be found blending their voices with the more acceptable arguments.

THE NAKED AND THE LED

Not long after a now famous *Vanity Fair* cover appeared on magazine racks, an *Evening Telegram* editor asked a number of us for a comment on the decision by Sobey's to withdraw the magazine from its stores because the actress, Demi Moore, appeared nude and very pregnant on the front cover. I found it hard to boil down my thoughts into a one-sentence reply, but I explained that while I didn't think the body of a pregnant women is anything but beautiful, I did object to it being used in an exploitative context. It seemed quite clear that the magazine cover was nothing more than a promotional gimmick guaranteed to produce a hit at the box office for the actress's new film.

I am not offended by depictions of naked bodies, but I am often offended by the way they are used.

The incident brought back a host of discussions that have taken place around the same kind of honest confusion. When is a portrayal demeaning and when is it merely a positive image of a woman? If it were in a magazine showing women's lives in a positive manner, it wouldn't raise an eyebrow—or not one of mine, anyway.

But if it is used to titillate to sell a product...well, I'm one of those feminists who is fed up with an advertising industry, let alone a pornography industry, that has cheapened women's body parts for profit.

When the current wave of the women's movement in Canada began in the sixties, there were still a lot of Victorian practices and ideas in circulation. A woman was identified through her relationship with a man; his name was the dominant one in most legal transactions. The roles for women were pretty restricted. Working outside the home was frowned upon, the role of wife and mother was considered aspiration enough for any woman, and if you weren't a married woman you were more to be pitied than censured.

If you did have a paying job, it was understood that you would work for less and follow only the professions that society determined suitable for the "weaker" sex. Nobody questioned the validity of marriage, or acknowledged that for some it might be unendurable. It was simply the highest state that women could reach for, and mothers and churches taught daughters early in life that they must learn not to complain but to accept their "natural" place in the scheme of things.

"Women's Libbers," as we were called, pointed out the unfairness of the narrow paths defined for women. Opposition was organized against the advertising industry that painted women as the bimbo, the dumb blond, the *hausfrau* who could only talk about cleaning her sink. Or the ideal that all women were supposed to aspire to—the sexpot who was also the obedient, self-sacrificing spouse who asked her husband how to vote. Women should be shown in positive images, we said.

We argued that pregnant women should not have to be kept in closets until the confinement was over, that nature and the body were treasures to be admired, not to be hidden or used as objectifying tools. We pointed to *Playboy*, then a new magazine, and said that the images presented there were demeaning to women.

But you know the end of that story as well as I do. *Playboy* went on to greater heights—or perhaps depths—and was joined by a noxious breed of very ugly and brutal magazines that delight in women's enslavement and, irony of ironies, are now defended on occasion by some of our most worthy citizens.

The women's movement went on to greater strengths, too, and doors have opened on many fronts. But the chains have not dropped away, and can be tightened at any time if we are uncaring. We've won the right to be natural. Pregnant women are seen now in all sorts of workplaces, and mothers feed their babies in public if they like without raising a storm by doing so.

It has always seemed so strange that in our culture a woman feeding a child from her breast can arouse embarrassment and sometimes even anger, but magazine racks—and in some places whole stores—can be devoted to the public display of women's breasts and bodies.

When my first child was but a few weeks old, I breastfed him at some friends' house while the four of us were discussing the new wonders of parenting. It took me a while to realize that the host, a teacher, had left the room in disgust, and I was annoyed at him all the way home. He was no stranger to breasts; his house held every *Playboy* magazine that had ever been printed, but that's what he thought was a proper display. It was many years later, after he had fathered a number of lovely daughters, that he was arrested for sexually assaulting a student. I've often thought that his story illustrates so well the brand of hypocrisy that we feminists find so objectionable.

But my favourite illustration of staggering hypocrisy is an event that occurred in Toronto around 1967. The city was abuzz with the talk of what was going on at city council. Charges had been laid against a couple whose children had been allowed to play nude on the beach at Centre Island. You're going to have trouble believing this, but the offensive children were the ripe old ages of two and four. Some councillors were enraged with their actions.

The picture in the local paper must have driven them further around the bend, for nothing could have been more endearing than these two little creatures, naked as the day they were born, playing with their buckets and sand castles under construction.

The discussions in the media and on council were endless. People took sides; the council stayed firm. There were unforgettable quotes: "They may get away with behaving like that in Europe but they'll not do it in Canada! Let them go back to where they've come from!"

Charges were upheld and fines levied on the parents for this un-Canadian act of depravity. In the same picture with the criminal toddlers was their mother, who was wearing a newly fashionable bikini, but there was no objection to that from the city council. Nor should there have been, of course, but it did underline the irony.

This city council was the same one that was issuing licenses for the innovative topless bars that had just started to emerge. They had no hesitation in granting a special license to the management of "Starvin' Marvin" to run strip shows for harried businessmen to enjoy with their soup and sandwich at lunch.

There is probably no area of experience as filled with contradictions as our attitudes to the human body. Isn't it about time we tried to sort it out?

ONLY IN CANADA?

As I drove down Duckworth Street one day, I noticed a man getting out of his car. Seeing him again brought back warm memories of a meeting we had many years ago on an Air Canada flight.

He was a provincial deputy minister at the time and was heading for Montreal, en route to civil-service heaven in Ottawa. I had to change planes in Halifax to continue on to Toronto, and as I passed down the aisle we nodded to each other in recognition. But moments later he caught up with me in the airport and explained he had got off the plane to comment on something I was involved in, so we talked for the half hour or so before he had to reboard.

He and his wife had watched a TV panel discussion that I had been on, and he said that it was only as they listened that he realized how difficult it was for the members of our Coalition Against Pornography to take a public stand against such a sordid industry. He realized that being a target for the people who like pornography, as well as the ones who like to profit from it, can't be much fun. He wanted us to know how much his family appreciated our efforts.

For me, it was like an antidote for mosquito bites. All the irritations of the struggle vanished with his kind words. And seeing him again the other day renewed the feeling of relief.

Porn has never been a subject that anyone in their right mind would choose to tangle with. Years ago, I would have slipped out the back door from our Women's Network Dinner when the Playboy film slated for Canadian television was about to be shown if the President of the Advisory Council on the Status of Women hadn't caught me in the act. She insisted that I stay and inform myself. But once informed you couldn't ignore the implications for society, particularly for youth.

Shortly before a recent federal election, a colleague and I appeared before the travelling committee on the issue of free trade. We argued on behalf of our Coalition of Citizens Against Pornography that if the free trade agreement went ahead, Canada would be opening its doors to the pornography industry. We talked about the huge difference between Canadian and American laws and contended that there would be an increase in violence to women and children if Canada followed the mandate of the free trade agreement. We would be interfering with the "free trade" of the porn industries if we insisted on having controlling laws.

John Crosbie, then Minister of Justice, scoffed "What are they talking about? There's nothing in the agreement about pornography." Of course not. But there was buried in the agreement something about the level playing field that would have to be achieved between the U.S. and Canada, and it was argued by those who opposed the free trade agreement that Canadian culture was included, that our laws would be forced to harmonize with the U.S. which meant lowering Canadian standards.

We argued that the Criminal Code of Canada provided a shield of protection that American women wished they had. Years ago when representatives of the National Action Committee on the Status of Women opposed in every province the distribution of an issue of *Penthouse*, we were extremely successful.

The magazine had a special section of photographs of young, nubile Japanese girls who were pictured in various stages of undress while tied, hanging to trees by their breasts, roped to boxcars, trussed with heavy hemp and, in a final picture, wearing a death mask. The man who pictured them in glossy purples and greys was one of the most renowned photographers in Japan.

We claimed that these portrayals threatened the safety of women, that our human rights were being denied by representations condoning bodily harm to women. In Newfoundland the magazines were prevented from distribution, but other provinces recalled the magazine from stores, which incited the publisher, Bob Guccione, to wild denunciations. He offered full-page advertisements of a huge swastika with the caption, "Only in Canada" to every leading newspaper, but only three printed it and one of these later apologized.

But we now have a free trade agreement. When did you last see an arrest for contravention of the criminal code regarding pornography?

During the free trade talks, Mulroney cronies liked to repeat scornfully that culture wasn't on the table. But since then we've seen one cultural institution slashed after another. Whether on the table or under the table, it is clear the corporate agenda wants to strip us of our cultural heritage.

In Marci McDonald's book, *Yankee Doodle Dandy*, Marcel Masse, who tried to be a good cultural minister, recounts some of his deepest disappointments. Every time he tried to get an omnibus bill passed ensuring protection of Canadian culture, cabinet support was withheld.

He laments to a reporter (p. 99) that "this country will disappear if we are more and more like the Americans," and explains that if you drop a frog in boiling water it will jump out, but if you start with cool water and gradually increase the heat, it won't know what has happened until it is cooked.

MOSES RAPS ROCK

Early in 1990, I was reading how Moses Znaimer, executive producer of the Much Music channel, had banned a video of a New York rap group called Public Enemy because he felt that it contains anti-Semitic attitudes.

It was good to learn that the station was also somewhat concerned about anti-black sentiment in some videos. And it was hard to disagree with Mr. Znaimer when he said that "there's a very negative side [to the music videos] emerging." The only word I'd argue with in that statement is the last one.

Mr. Znaimer made a plea for understanding. "Banning is a hard-line stand for us, he said." However, "In Public Enemy's case, the evidence of anti-Semitism is conclusive." Paul Burger, President of CBS Records Canada, added his assurance that "We are committed to making sure that none of our records promote bigotry."

Well, bully for them. There is one little problem, though. They don't seem to have noticed that ever since Much Music came on the air, it has been playing videos in which another group of people has been demeaned, degraded and attacked. I rather see that as a form of bigotry too. Anytime you care to flick on the TV you can see women being chained, strangled, threatened and sexually humiliated. Of course, it is all pretty impartial from a racial and religious point of view. It doesn't seem to matter whether the women are black, white, Jewish, Christian, or whatever—they all get the same treatment.

As long ago as May 12, 1984, an article in the *Montreal Gazette* by Brenda Zosky Proulx described the videos then playing on Canadian television as showing "scenes of murder, torture, terror, hostility, sexual aggression and entirely sexist sexuality."

She provided a few examples: a naked woman struggling in chains behind a translucent sheet while the male singer suggestively sharpens a straight razor... a female singer changes from a man-pleasing blonde to a leather-clad punker and ends up strangled to death... bare-breasted women rub their bodies along a whipped-cream-covered pole, then wrestle in mud...a woman showers behind a curtain while a knife appears and plunges toward her body... Michael Jackson achieves ecstasy by terrorizing his girlfriend.

And it hasn't got any better in the years since. The videos show a steady diet of women in chains, women in cages, women harnessed like animals, women writhing in submission at the feet of powerful males.

Thomas Radecki, a psychiatrist from the University of Illinois, was quoted in the 1984 *Gazette* story as saying that American law prevents a person from giving a speech that would incite violence, but seems to allow the most gruesome sadism to be presented as entertainment. "People play back the messages they receive on rock videos over and over in their minds. And if they are violent it can be harmful." He continued: "The disgusting and destructive nature of rock videos parallels the dramatic increase in sadistic violence in pornography. Much of it is aimed at women...24-hour rock video stations are out to guarantee that the second television generation will be more violent than the first, which turned out to be the most violent generation of Americans on record."

At the time a spokesman for Much Music said that critics of the violence were simply not attuned to the moment. Dennis Fitzgerald of City-TV was quoted as saying, "I will be candid. No two ways about it, I think a lot of adults find some of the material in the clips offensive. I think that's part of the attraction, and it has been the same throughout history."

I can't help wondering how many of these videos Marc Lepine enjoyed during the six years that preceded his killing of fourteen women in Montreal.

By banning a video, Mr. Znaimer risked running the ire of the Canadian Civil Liberties Association, and various artistic and literary groups. They certainly took up the cudgel when some of us called for controls on violent pornography. I fully expected a large-scale, well-financed campaign to take up the issue of Much Music employing censorship against the beleaguered Public Enemy. And I wondered what further displays could we look forward to by libertarians proclaiming freedom for the arts?

9 Some of My Best Friends

Support for equality issues does not always divide along gender lines. There are loads of men who would like to live in a world where women's voices counted. I hear from them regularly, both young and old. And sometimes, too, I hear from angry women who support the status quo and who want nothing to do with feminists.

HAPPY FATHER'S DAY

In my writing, I usually concentrate on celebrating the work and contribution of women. However, we should not lose sight of the fact that over the years a lot of men have contributed to the struggle for simple justice for women. The modern women's movement has fathers as well as mothers, and what better time to acknowledge them than on the eve of Father's Day?

One of the best known in his time was the eminent British philosopher, John Stuart Mill, who in 1867 proposed a bill to the British parliament calling for women's suffrage. Two years later, Mr. Mill published an essay entitled "The Subjection of Women" that is still a landmark in the literature on women's equality.

His contemporary, the feminist Olive Schreiner, probably overdid things a little when she described him as the "noblest of those whom the English speaking race has produced in the last hundred years," but we can sympathize with what sounds like desperation in those words and agree with her further statement: "We shall have to learn the lesson Mill taught—that the freedom of all human creatures is essential to the full development of human life on earth."

The book, *Woman Suffrage in Canada*, by Catherine L. Cleverdon, provides many examples of men who helped in that historic struggle. There was Dr. James Hughes of Toronto, for example, who pored over old and new testaments to produce a pamphlet that once and for all put an end to any serious debate on whether there were Biblical reasons for denying women the vote. Across Canada many Protestant clergy not only gave sermons in support of the franchise but also accompanied women's groups making presentations to parliament.

I was surprised to learn that the first organization in Canada explicitly devoted to gaining the vote for women, the Equal Franchise League of Edmonton, was headed by a man, Dr. W.H. Alexander.

Official labour organizations played a supportive role. In 1912 the British Columbia Federation of Labour, which must have been largely male, passed a resolution calling for women's suffrage. Labour was also active in Manitoba and Ontario. In New Brunswick, the sponsor of a 1913 suffrage bill pointed out that it was backed not only by the local suffrage society and the Women's Christian Temperance Union but also by the Carpenters' and Joiners' Brotherhood of Saint John, a group that could hardly have included many women.

The most outstanding support in Canada, however, occurred in the prairie provinces with the help given by the Farmers' Associations who were determined allies of the cause. According to Catherine Cleverdon, "these farmers did more than pay lip service as they joined their women in petitions and delegations, and carried the idea of equality into their own organizations by admitting women to full membership."

Their official organ, the *Grain Growers' Guide*, began a crusade for the vote for women. The editor, George Chipman, placed an ardent suffragist in charge of the women's page which became a forum for the dissemination of suffrage news and ideas. Little wonder that Manitoba was the first province to grant women's suffrage.

It was fascinating, too, to learn that when the first stirrings began in Manitoba in 1890, it was a group of Icelandic women who founded the pioneer suffrage movement, which later included both women and men. Feminists in Newfoundland have made warm connections with the women's movement in Iceland in recent times, so it was an exciting discovery to find that our history had already forged a feminist link.

Acting Premier T.H. Johnson, the son of an Icelandic suffrage pioneer, had the pleasure of marking the historic moment for women when he gave third reading of the franchise bill to the Manitoba legislature. It must have been a great moment. The vote was unanimous and the chamber broke into an uproar.

Men on the floor of the legislature stood up to sing in unison with the women in the packed galleries, "for they are jolly good fellows." It is not clear whether they were singing about themselves or whether they were including women as honourary fellows, but there is no question that their hearts were in the right place.

Women had supporters in Newfoundland too. In spite of opposition from Prime Minister Squires, other men were actively giving support to women's suffrage. One of them deserves special mention, not only because of his support but because he was a father not only in domestic, but also in political life, as a Father of Confederation.

In a letter to *The Evening Telegram* on June 27, 1921, a young man named J. R. Smallwood wrote:

> I am pained beyond measure to read in this morning's News that Mr. J. A. MacDonnell is still an anti-suffragist, and that he still `strenuously opposes' the suffrage bill. I really thought that I had converted him...Of course `women's place is in her home'—if she has one to be in. Voting in this country occurs once every four years, and takes about three minutes to accomplish. Roughly, an hour every four years will be totally wasted by women having the vote. I can sympathize with Mr. MacDonnell's apprehension over this fact. Terrible possibilities are wrapped up in it.
>
> I close now with the suggestion that the place for the girl stenographers, and office workers of Mr. MacDonnell's office is in the home—will he live up to his principle?

In Newfoundland as in Canada, many newspaper publishers and editors were strong allies of the women's cause. Cleverdon quotes an anonymous writer of the day who said, "Men like the Honourable John Alexander Robinson, M.B.E., owner of the *Daily News*, was our greatest friend and adviser. He published all we sent in and gave us many editorials as well...W. J. Herder threw open the columns of his paper, *The Evening Telegram*, and did all in his power to help our cause." And, of course, the legislative bodies that finally passed women's suffrage bills were made up of men.

The struggle for the vote was a neat, clear-cut issue. Many of the issues the women's movement is dealing with today are much more complex, much harder to see in black and white. But there are still plenty of jolly good fellows out there giving us support. Among them are the men who fight against demeaning images of women in pornography, the fathers who teach their children that daughters are as worthy as sons, and the husbands who support their wives in pursuing their own interest and careers.

Thanks fellows (and especially one fellow). Don't think you're not appreciated. Happy Father's Day.

MEDIA MEN

One of my favourite columnists is Stewart MacLeod, whose reading of the political pulse frequently finds agreement from me. That is, it did until a short time ago. That's when he took pot shots at Audrey McLaughlin. The honeymoon is over as far as Audrey's performance in the House of Commons goes, MacLeod said, and the boys in the media aren't impressed. Well here we go again, I thought. We've seen this before.

Ed Broadbent got similar treatment when he took over the NDP leadership from David Lewis. The pundits doubted that he would ever be able to come close to the stature of his predecessor. Robert Stanfield was criticized and ridiculed—always holding a banana—and presented as bumbling and inept from the day he won the Conservative leadership. Joe Clark was "Joe Who?" and every one of his—admittedly numerous—gaffes was gleefully seized upon. The boys in the media liked Trudeau; sliding down bannisters made good copy.

And later? Ed Broadbent ended up as the most respected politician in the country. Joe Clark was recently described as the only statesman in the Mulroney cabinet. And once he had been hounded out of office, the media allowed us to see Mr. Stanfield in truer colours as an intelligent and witty man. Mr. Trudeau eventually faded from the scene without too many tears.

In all these cases the media were reacting to style rather than substance. The men they didn't give a passing grade to brought a style that was different from what the press corps was used to—or approved of—and they got the chop.

Women politicians have an extra cross to bear unless they fit into the time-worn shape of the male of the same species. If a woman has a strong voice, and interrupts a lot, and shouts, and dominates the scene, the media will approve and recognize that she knows how to play the game. She will have got over the first hurdle. We're all used to that cut and thrust style, and we react to what is familiar. But if women are to take their place in politics, then we're going to have to make adjustments in our expectations as to both style and substance.

Most women have softer voices than men. Most women have grown up as listeners and not interrupters. Women's culture stresses co-operation and giving turns. It is less competitive and combative. Female politicians may well stress the importance of social issues that rarely make it to the top of the list of male politicians. They might even show emotion on issues like daycare.

Teachers in the three St. John's Roman Catholic high schools which have become co-educational have told me that they much prefer mixed classes of boys and girls. They are easier to work with and much more pleasant, they say. Studies have shown that, in classrooms where girls are in the majority, there is much less competition and much more cooperation. Could we dare to hope that such a civilizing influence could take place in the parliaments of our country?

The trail blazers will have the worst of it. There aren't any courses that I know of to inform the Stuart MacLeods and all the other media boys that you have to listen differently if you're going to adjudicate what women politicians can bring to the national scene.

In 1984 the National Action Committee on the Status of Women sponsored the first—and only, so far—national debate on women's issues with all three federal party leaders present. After seeing at first hand the response from the national media, I came away from the meeting realizing that somehow the stranglehold of male opinion makers had to be broken if women were ever to have fair press. It wasn't that they were malicious; it was just that the male pundits were so used to their own style of asking questions that they couldn't cope with the change. They expected women to act like men, as though their practices were the only ones possible.

But on this unique event, it was different. Women were calling the shots on format and rules, and the gentlemen of the press were not happy. They were critical and dismissive and not one of them seemed to realize that they were witnessing an event of worldwide importance. No other country has had a debate like it before or since.

When the Meech Lake submissions were being made in St. John's, a friend of mine was clearly impressed with the Liberal MP from the Northwest Territories who spoke sincerely, quietly and, if you listened, powerfully. Ethel Blondin was pointing out that she was discriminated against three times under Meech, as a woman, as a native and as a northerner. My friend added "of course, she was nervous but she'll soon get over that."

Later I thought about what he had said. Nervousness was a fair way of putting it, but it's more than that, I think. The MP was responding as a lot of women do to a male forum where the rigid rules aren't ours and are meant to be intimidating. We're not happy with the combative "win or lose" mentality. My guess is that she wasn't nervous about making her contribution so much as she was responding negatively to the hostile climate that existed around that table.

But let's get back to Stuart MacLeod who claims there's no sex bias because women reporters are just as critical of Audrey as the male ones. Some women in the media are no different from their male counterparts. They've either voluntarily learned or had to accept the system that operates, in order to move up the ladder. Some, maybe many, would like to make changes but have learned not to try.

I saw an occasion of this when the Provincial Advisory Council on the Status of Women made its presentation to the Meech Lake committee. The national media, including at least one well-known woman commentator, got up and walked out for a smoke and only came back when the five women presenters were finished. Why cover the words of women? The editor would cut it anyway. They missed a jewel of a moment when Robert Kaplan, MP, actually asked our women representatives if they were willing to take the responsibility for Canada coming apart. We've been blamed for everything else so why not for Meech as well?

So my advice to women is to go on bringing a women's style of democratization to a parliament sorely in need of it. Sooner or later wise old Stewart MacLeod is bound to catch on.

MORE THAN JUST A GOVERNOR

In writing of Co-ops a while ago, I looked up a book that was given to me when I was very young, entitled *A Poor Man's Prayer*, by George Boyle. It's the story of the Credit Union movement and while I simply intended to check on a fact or two I became once again enthralled by the story.

One of the strong political and economic forces in Quebec has been the "Caisse Populaire," the Credit Union movement. It was started in the early years of this century by Alphonse Desjardins, who had a dream that working-class people could operate their own savings and loan societies. He had been a newspaperman and later a stenographer in the House of

Commons and became obsessed with the possibility of improving life for the people around him.

Desjardins argued that, though working people had very little money, together it amounted to something substantial and could provide the basis on which a loan society could operate for the good of the community. Farms and businesses had been lost because loan sharks had either refused working people credit or charged them such outrageous interest that they could never get out from under the debt. But their own Caisse could make loans on humane considerations and on the mutual respect that members held for each other.

M. Desjardins gave his life to the formation of this dream and so did his family. His home became the office, handling the accounts, keeping the books. Often he was called away and, though he looked for replacements, there was but one person he could count on: his wife, Doriméne

Neighbours had uncertainties. Would they lose their tiny deposits? Would people pay back their loans? Could they swallow their pride and ask for a loan from people they knew?

The local priest became an ardent Caisse supporter. In the book, Boyle has him explaining to Archbishop Bégin, "In my parish, people are born, grow up, and go away. It is the same with the wealth. What is produced there goes out. Life goes out of there. We export life. Our parish is a harvest for outside entrepreneurs. Must our people become road walkers and migrants in the land that their ancestors tamed? Simply because their worldly and alert fellow citizens have learned the secrets of controlling and managing business?"

The Archbishop pledged his full support which greatly influenced the House of Commons to pass a limited liability bill making it possible for credit unions to operate. But the Senate rejected the bill by one vote, on the grounds that it was a provincial matter.

Monopolies and financial interests were mounting strong opposition. They did not take kindly to a system of neighbour helping neighbour, and their campaign to destroy the movement was ruthless in spreading falsehoods and rumours. But in the end the good guys won. In 1906, Quebec passed the bill that became known as the Quebec Syndicates Act, and the federal government set up a parliamentary committee of inquiry to review the issue.

The committee called forth a most unusual witness: it must have stunned the populace to see the Governor General of Canada appearing before the inquiry like any other ordinary citizen, and it must have been even more surprising to hear him extolling the virtues of the Caisse Populaire. This man was more than just another governor.

Earl Grey, whose name we connect today with both the tea and the famous cup, had become a member of the Caisse Populaire in Levis, across the river from his Quebec City residence. He had gone over the books with M. Desjardins, and was delighted to see that all loans had been paid back and that accounts were kept in good order. He knew of the success of credit unions in Europe and understood the needs of the people to have access to credit on fair terms. He took his stand on the side of working people.

Grey had been secretary to Queen Victoria and, when appointed to Canada, gave a rip-roaring speech in Halifax that according to the press "caught the imagination of Canadians" and marked him as a reformer. He maintained: "If you keep the character of your people high, virile, heroical...no one can venture to set the limits of influence of the Canadian nation." It's hard to imagine a Governor General taking such a strong stand today. Where are these heroes now that we need them?

SPRINGTIME IN STEPHENVILLE

Some people go to Lourdes to get renewal; others go to a health spa or to some place in the sun where they find peace of mind. I go to the west coast of Newfoundland, to Stephenville.

That's where I get—not exactly peace of mind, but something even more therapeutic—the recharging of my feminist batteries. I always come back rejuvenated, with excitement and a renewal of hope that it is possible to achieve a world where children are protected, where men and women walk as equal partners and where this abused old planet can yet be rescued from the environmental disasters of the past.

Coming back from a week of speaking and learning in the Bay St. George region, I talked into the wee hours, recalling for my patient husband the incredible story of the outreach work of the Women's Centre and other agencies in Stephenville.

The Centre has been a focal point in that area in providing women with access to help on any number of problems, and a haven for young people who are running away from, or confronting, the violence in their lives. Help and support has been given from within the women's community and in cooperation with other agencies working in Stephenville and environs.

Over the years the Centre has provided speakers for public debates and discussions on issues of concern. Their representatives have met with almost every key organization in the region to talk about issues of equality, to raise consciousness and insight. Workshops have been held on a continuing basis with young and old. Information on feminist perspectives has been provided to schools, the Community College and community groups. The Centre has sponsored discussions for parents, teachers and church leaders. It has offered a program for offenders from the penitentiary whereby violent men learn something about human relationships at the same time that they learn the fundamentals of cooking. The raised consciousness and positive results from all this community interaction is easy to see.

Stephenville is a town where people work together. They seem able to put differences aside as they work for the good of the community. This is expressed in many different ways, sometimes by volunteers working their heads off for the highly successful annual drama festival; at another time by the well-organized committee working on environmental concerns, bringing citizens together for cleanups of the beaches, teaching them the sad and necessary skills of how to clean shore birds that have been trapped and covered in oil.

A new library was under construction, and I was told in a matter-of-fact way that residents had found the money by fund-raising projects as though that's what happens everywhere. I would be hard pressed to find a similar community endeavour in the capital city of St. John's.

I don't want to leave the impression that Stephenville is synonymous with heaven. There are—as in every community—severe problems of violence and child abuse that must be dealt with. What is different is the mutual understanding and the commitment of community agencies to bring an end to the problem.

Key institutions in that region show a general acceptance that the oppression women have faced has been one of the major contributing factors to problems of child abuse and wife battering.

The frustration that social agencies live with on a daily basis in trying to find the answers is shared by those who work at the Women's Centre. They have brought together police, members of the judiciary, teachers, church representatives and the town council. The Centre has helped people on both sides of the law, the inmates and their victims.

Key ministries—Education, Status of Women, Social Services, Justice and Health—are cooperating with Stephenville and Bay St. George agencies in developing plans to make the region the safe place it deserves to be.

The most moving moment of one visit was listening to a videotaped speech by Stephenville Mayor Cecil Stein given in his chambers on International Women's Day. He referred to the women's symbolic quilt, loaned to the town council for the occasion by Wendy Williams and the Advisory Council on the Status of Women, as being an entirely appropriate symbol for the occasion because it represented "womanhood, motherhood and childhood... and add to that their idea of a society based on peace, equality and justice, isn't that what the Status of Women is all about?"

Mayor Stein reacted strongly when he saw government cutting off finances to the women's council and spending more than 120 million dollars over budget for the Museum of Civilization. In his words:

> Then your struggles are not over. When I see a government cutting back money on health and education...then your struggles are not over.
> When I see a government saying to municipalities that it will no longer give a grant on behalf of social assistance recipients to the town...then your struggles are not over. When I see a government that will not bow its head for a minute of silence for a just cause, then your struggle is not over. For it is not who is right but what is right... Many of your causes are all so difficult... Hold fast to your dreams... Equality will only come through your own personal efforts. If you believe that then never give up. Never give up.

The Mayor's words represent a growing breed of men who are not afraid of the word feminist nor afraid to be counted on the side of equality. His words and the example of his community bring a renewal of hope.

The town itself just keeps knitting together, sharing resources, tackling problems. The Bay St. George Women's Centre hosted a rousingly successful conference in 1995 that drew 200 delegates from across the province. They followed that event a few weeks later with a "Take Back the Night" march on December 6 to commemorate the Montreal Massacre. Hundreds joined in to mourn the deaths of the fourteen women and to work for change.

10 And We Thought We'd Got Rid of Brian

Following in the footsteps of Reagan and Thatcher, Mulroney has thrust a new pro-business conservatism on Canada. But, unlike Reagan and Thatcher, who were up-front about their plans, Mulroney has been sneaky, like a man trying to seduce a woman he has no real interest in.
Linda McQuaig, *The Quick and the Dead*

IN BED WITH AN ELEPHANT

It has been said that those who don't know their history are condemned to relive it. It never seemed truer than when I viewed the National Film Board's "In Bed With an Elephant"—an apt title for a discussion on the free trade issue.

It is staggering to see how many times in history one man makes a decision that is binding on a nation. The unbelievable ego of an individual who believes that not only does he have the divine right to rule but is also gifted with the divine ability to always know what is right! Why do parliaments, to this very day, still allow all this power to be vested in one man?

The film takes us back to the beginning of Canada and shows us the strange realignments of our national ruling parties over the years. There was a time, we are reminded, when Conservative meant conserving that which is Canadian. The fight for Canadian sovereignty has been a bitter and continuous struggle.

Sir John A. MacDonald and John Diefenbaker must be churning in their graves these days to see the turn-around of the present Conservatives.They fought hard to maintain an independent Canada and strenuously opposed free trade, knowing that it would be the beginning of an eventual assimilation of mouseland into elephantland. That, of course, was also the position of Brian Mulroney until he was elected with a far too comfortable majority.

Prime Minister MacKenzie King, in breaking away from British colonial powers, was enormously attracted to the American ways of his former employer, John D. Rockefeller. He ingratiated himself into becoming an intimate friend of President Franklin Roosevelt who considered King an amusing fellow. His wife, Eleanor Roosevelt, did not. She considered King to be loathsome.

King, in fawning admiration, began secret talks with Roosevelt about free trade and didn't even share his plans with his own cabinet. It seems he had second thoughts later, and in 1948 became alarmed, remembering the defeat of Laurier over the same issue, so he burned all his papers on the subject.

The Diefenbaker administration was determined to stay free of American domination but paid a price for being a government with a mind of its own. Those were the years when Canada pursued at least a measure of independent foreign policy. Our country gave "Red China," as it was called then, official recognition in spite of the American embargo that was in place. We sold China our prairie wheat and President Kennedy threatened to block the shipments. The same was true for Cuba where trade relations continued between our country and theirs, despite U.S. condemnation.

Diefenbaker's External Affairs Minister, Howard Green, won the admiration of people outside of his party for his stalwart stand in opposing nuclear warheads in Canada. The strong, independent and fiercely nationalist stand taken by the Canadian government made the U.S. indignant. When Kennedy couldn't budge Diefenbaker, he set out to help in his defeat. Kennedy's Democrats even sent top strategists to Canada to help the Liberal Party win the election.

But there's a price to be paid whether you stand up to the elephant or submit to its wishes. Diefenbaker's government went down to defeat. Lester Pearson and the Liberals came to power, but their victory was somewhat tarnished when they knuckled under to U.S. pressure and allowed nuclear warheads to be placed on Canadian soil. The prime minister, after all, had been awarded a Nobel prize sometime earlier for his work for peace and for his adamant opposition to the warheads. But that kind of caving in is only the beginning when you deal with elephants.

Former cabinet minister in the Pearson government, Walter Gordon, told the story of Pearson being summoned, not *asked*, to come immediately to Washington by President Lyndon Johnson. Pearson had angered the President by giving a speech denouncing the war in Vietnam. Walter Gordon described the meeting in Washington where an angry and violent Lyndon Johnson picked up our prime minister by the throat and shook him, while uttering epithets at his daring to speak up to the U.S. government. It's hard to accept the grovelling that went with it, but the film quotes the letter Pearson wrote after returning home, thanking Johnson for "your kindness, your consideration for speaking to me so frankly."

There's a hefty price for dependence or independence. I guess it boils down to which price you're willing to pay.

The Pearson years saw a growth of the branch plant economy into Canada where more and more businesses were owned by American companies. President of the Economic Council of Canada, Stuart Smith, interviewed in the film, describes this period as a time when foreign domination meant that American branch plants that had no allegiance to Canada simply saw our country as an extension of their markets and had no respect for Canadian laws or traditions.

Minister Walter Gordon begged the cabinet to see that foreign ownership of our economy was disastrous. He couldn't persuade *them* but was perfectly understood by the U.S. foreign secretary, John Foster Dulles. He was quoted as saying "there are two ways to control a country, one is by war and the other is by economics."

Near the end of the film Walter Gordon comments on today's free trade issues and says that surely everyone today must realize that when the "business community" is quoted as saying it supports free trade, it isn't Canadian business that is talking. It is the managers and executives of American branch plant companies.

Gordon hasn't lost hope for the future of Canada. He says, "If Canadians have the will to survive (as Canadians) then of course we will. If people don't care, then we could be lost."

Narrator James Laxer sums up with the comment that Canada must be the only country in the world that has to fight anew for its sovereignty every ten years or so. Broadcaster David Halton, speaking from Washington, describes Mulroney as the most pro-American prime minister that Canada ever had.

Funny—it used to be that people who defended their country against foreign domination were called patriots. There was a less flattering term for those who sold out.

NOT ANOTHER FREE (YOU MUST BE KIDDING) TRADE AGREEMENT

It was 1993. We were getting primed for another federal election, and with another trade agreement in the works. The public relations companies and ad agencies were rubbing their hands in glee.

The first time we were sold free trade, the Tories and their corporate friends spent an estimated $50 million trying to convince Canadians that the Free Trade Agreement would be wonderful. We were treated to the endlessly repeated message that the FTA would make our markets larger, create opportunities, and remove restrictive barriers. It would bring jobs, jobs, jobs.

Opponents argued that it would *lose* jobs, jobs, jobs and that what was at stake was Canada; this wasn't a trade agreement so much as a sellout of the country. The famous "level playing field" dreamed up by those expensive PR people would mean that we would have to reduce our standards of social programming. Medicare, family allowance, Canada pension, old age security and unemployment insurance would have to decline to the much lower U.S. levels.

Proponents laughed at such paranoia and reminded us that the Prime Minister himself had promised that our social programs were sacred trusts. Could we doubt his word?

Analysts like *Canadian Forum* writer Ed Finn weren't persuaded. Ed said that trade would not be free and neither would Canada. He maintained that Canada has been a much more caring society than the U.S. and that, as just one example of what would happen under the FTA, our system of reducing regional disparity by equalization grants to the poorer provinces would be regarded by the U.S. as unfair competition. Ed, as a Newfoundlander, knew how important those payments are to eastern provinces particularly. He prophesied, long before the 1993 election, that Canada could lose up to 600,000 jobs if the Free Trade Agreement were allowed to stand.

Dr. Marjorie Bowker, a judge from Alberta whom most of us had never heard of, warned that Canada would lose control of its natural resources, that American takeovers of Canadian businesses would occur with no terms or conditions imposed as to their operation, that our sovereignty would be threatened, with ownership and control of Canadian industry gravitating to the United States. "Decision making will be transferred to the boardrooms of New York and Washington," she said. "Political power is known to eventually follow the movement of economic power...Canada could face the eventual loss of political independence, and its sovereignty as a nation."

Even the Grocery Products Manufacturers of Canada said, "Canadian workers' income expectations will have to be substantially lowered." The Canadian Teachers Federation said there would be "increasing pressure [on our school system] to conform more closely to their generally less adequately funded and less equitable U.S. counterparts."

Well, who was right?

What we have seen are federal cutbacks to the provinces and territories in the fields of education and health. Equalization payments are being phased out. National programs are either being demolished as with the family allowance, or weakened as with medicare.

And jobs? Well, it depends on who you believe, but some analysts consider Ed Finn's 600,000 to be pretty close to how many Canadian jobs have disappeared as one company after another has moved south of the border. You can argue the numbers back and forth, but what is inarguable is that Canada now has the worst rate of unemployment since the Great Depression. Branch plant companies have closed up shop in Canada and moved south. An estimated ten thousand businesses have moved out of Canada.

In 1993, we witnessed another sellout in the works, this time to drug companies, as Bill C-91 worked its way through parliament and Senate hearings. Watchers of the Bill knew that, if it passed, our drug prices, which were one-third lower on average than those in the U.S., would increase. Provincial health plans would lose billions of dollars over the next decade, making it all the easier for a big-business government to cut them back.

Our two airlines, de-regulated according to the U.S. model, had to battle it out. Canadian had to consider, as a last hope, selling out a major piece of the operation to American Airlines.

Transportation systems are a country's life blood. To sell them off to foreigners is madness. Anybody care to guess how much priority an American-owned airline would give to stops in Stephenville or Labrador

City? And how would we get to Toronto or Vancouver? By way of New York, Detroit, and Chicago?
What emerged from free trade was a gloomy scenario. And there was worse to come.

Of course, Mulroney's drug bill passed easily. His original monopoly gift to the pharmaceutical companies was bumped up from seven to ten years for patent protection, to seventeen to twenty years.
Marci McDonald, author of *Yankee Doodle Dandy*, reported that:

> ...within three years of its passage, the cost of prescription drugs had almost doubled to $1.9 billion, wreaking havoc with provincial budgets (p.212).

And she writes of what followed after the 1993 federal election:

> For nearly two years, Canadian voters drifted on a tide of wilful euphoria. They had done it—delivered such a stunning rebuke not only to Mulroney's anointed heir, Kim Campbell, but, in the process, to his entire agenda that they had shattered the Conservative Party into a two-seat curiosity washed up on the margins of parliament (p. 360).

It took that long before Canadians realized that the little guy from Shawinigan was following the same agenda as his hated predecessor.

Prime Minister Chrétien signed us up to the North American Free Trade Agreement (NAFTA) and picked his previously most-leaning-to-the-left member of cabinet, Lloyd Axworthy, to be the henchman for the new Liberal ultra-right-wing policies. Lloyd came out swinging. Social programs didn't stand a chance. Cultural institutions were brought to their knees. The big Ax stood in defence of banks and bondholders. Mulroney congratulated Mr. Chrétien for having more courage than he had had.

"How the Liberals Abandoned the Just Society" is described by Maude Barlow and Bruce Campbell in their book, *Straight Through The Heart*.

> The reinvention of Canada under the Liberals and those provincial governments who share their view is a return to the bad old days: good services for the wealthy, what's left over for the rest—means-

testing, impoverished public schools and public hospitals, relief camps, food banks...Not even health care is safe.

Why hasn't there been more outcry. Ed Finn has some thoughts about that:

> Observing the barrage of anger, resentment and hate now being hurled against people on welfare, I'm reminded of the old African proverb: *'As the waterhole gets smaller, the animals get meaner.'* As the basic resources diminish, in other words, so does the willingness to share.
> So do the qualities of tolerance and neighbourliness. The sense of community is replaced by an ugly survival-of-the-fittest mentality... Our economic and social waterhole, in short, is getting smaller—is being coldly and callously *made* smaller.
> So far we have responded predictably by getting meaner. It's time we got smarter.

ELECTION FRIGHT

I have seen and taken part in more elections than I care to count, but the quietest one I ever saw was the election of 1993. It wasn't that people didn't care, but they seemed paralyzed—disillusioned—close to despair. There was no heat to speak of, and even less light.

And yet it might have been the most important election in Canada's history. It could have been the election that would mark the loss of our unity, the destruction of our sovereignty, and the abandonment of the social principles that have made this one of the best places in the world to live.

Why was everyone so quiet?

There used to be an understanding that Canadians wanted to share the wealth of the country, that full employment was a goal we all adhered to, that taxes would be progressive with the rich paying their full share. Then things changed, especially in the Mulroney years. We ignore the evidence at our peril. Try to imagine this battered province of Newfoundland without UI, with cut-down pensions and costly medical care.

The corporate agenda had brought us to a sorry pass by the time of the 1993 election. At the "great" debate we saw the lone defender of social programs, Audrey McLaughlin, pitted against four people who, one way or another, would like to dismantle the things that make Canada what it is:

the Liberal leader, Jean Chrétien, speaking for the right wing of his party, two ex-Mulroney Cabinet Ministers, Lucien Bouchard for the Bloc Quebecois and Kim Campbell for the Tories and an ex-Social Krediter, now Reformer, Preston Manning who viewed the other three as too far to the left.

Kim Campbell had been a cabinet minister in two of the most right wing governments in the history of Canada; Vander Zalm's in B.C. and Mulroney's in Ottawa. Neither was noted for equality in distributing the wealth. As Osgoode Hall law professor Neil Brooks observes,

> People at the right end of the ideological spectrum see a world in which each of us is responsible for himself or herself. People on the left see a world in which we are to a significant degree responsible for one another.

We can thank our lucky stars that Canada's grass-roots movements fought and won the early battles for universal pensions and equality in health care and education. But try to picture the Canada of the future without our safety net. Who would look after your aged parents? Would the rich be once again the only ones able to afford costly operations and drugs? Would children go without food and education? Would universities cater only to the wealthy, excluding the daughters and sons of fishermen and fisherwomen? Who would keep the small stores operating if people had their minimal securities cut back? Without medicare the women's movement couldn't exist. We'd be back to scrambling just to keep our loved ones looked after.

Tommy Douglas, the father of medicare, must be turning in his grave. He used to warn us to fight the very first incursion into medicare; the cutbacks, the user fees, the two-tier systems. Tommy fought the hold of the drug companies and would have been outraged by government giveaways that have cost our hospitals millions of dollars.

We have been bombarded by government and media messages telling us that we have no choices: that we must cut back on social spending if we are to compete in the global marketplace. In her book *The Wealthy Banker's Wife*, journalist Linda McQuaig pleads with us to look at the contrary evidence and know that we don't have to follow the American example of a country that has a comfortable elite and impoverished masses. McQuaig gives impressive examples of western European nations that have both vibrant economies and strong social welfare systems.

Indeed, how could an economy be described as vibrant if it didn't ensure job security and equality in human development?
Trent University political scientist Robert Campbell says:

> The biggest danger we face as a society is the view that we have no choices to make—the view that we have to accept, as inevitable, every new dictate of technology and every pressure from the international market.... Collectively, we can deal with those pressures and still have choices and social goals.... We can only do this together if we remember what the purpose of life is. The purpose of life is not profit. It's having a humanely happy community, where persons can use their gifts and can care about others, and can thrive.

That's what was at stake in the 1993 federal election. It will be at stake in the next election too.

The Fraser and C.D. Howe (corporate) Institutes and their friends in the media love to spread the myth about New Zealand "hitting a debt wall." Canadians are supposed to be so terrorized with this grim story that we will allow the Chretien bulldozers to run over our social programs with scarcely a whimper.

Journalist Linda McQuaig writes that the story of the debt wall is a myth, but contends that it is true that the New Zealand experience has relevance for Canada:

> ...eight years of stringent monetarist policies [in New Zealand] have produced massive unemployment, rising crime rates, a widening gap between rich and poor and a declining GDP.
> *Shooting the Hippo*,
> (Death by Deficit and Other Canadian Myths)

CHOPPING SOCIAL PROGRAMS

In 1994, as the federal government planned to chop up Canada's social programs, Lloyd Axworthy said he didn't expect too much opposition to the proposed changes, at least not from right-thinking citizens. The only difficulty he expected was from "special interest groups."

The same year, while the New Democratic Party was meeting to discuss its future, Rex Murphy had a crew of disgruntled party hacks on Cross Country Check-up to tell us where the party had gone wrong. Rex and his motley panel agreed that the blame falls squarely on... guess who? Right the first time. Special Interest Groups.

Others had been pointing out the wickedness of SIGs, and it was a real eye-opener to me. You see, all this time I had been naive enough to believe that politics is a kind of contest between groups with different interests, and that political parties and politicians support, and are supported by, different groups. I also believed that it was the duty of a citizen to engage in politics to try to make things better for people who were having a rough time. But I can see now that I was wrong.

I used to think that a national unemployment insurance system was put in place in 1941 because the economic system wasn't providing enough jobs, and a lot of people were suffering. And that a universal old-age pension was adopted because a lot of people, after a lifetime of hard work, did not have enough to live on. And that we got medicare because the existing system was so grossly unfair, and that things like universal suffrage and matrimonial property acts and pay equity were brought in because finally people were able to understand that women were being systematically discriminated against. I even used to think that these were good things, things we all ought to be proud of.

Now, though, thanks to Lloyd and Rex and the others, I can see that these were all products of the dreaded Special Interest Groups. We have to undo their evil works, and from now on governments and political parties, including the NDP, must formulate policy without regard for any particular group of people, no matter how much they moan and complain.

Mind you, it is going to take me a while to get onto the details of this new way of thinking. One thing I am having a bit of difficulty with is figuring out just who is a Special Interest Group and who isn't.

For instance, in 1992 a teller in a Royal Bank in B.C. earned about $25,000.00, and paid about $5,700.00 in tax. The Royal Bank made a profit of $63 million, and paid no tax at all. Now, as I understand it, if the tellers got together and complained about the taxation system, they would be a Special Interest Group and we should not pay any attention to them. The chartered banks, on the other hand, are not a Special Interest Group—unless they get together and complain about not paying enough taxes. If they did that, they would be a SIG, and we shouldn't listen to them, either.

You can see how complicated it is, but I think that's the way it goes.

Or take seasonal workers who do the only jobs available for as long as they are available, and then go on Unemployment Insurance. If they object to being pushed off UI and onto welfare, well, what can you expect from a

Special Interest Group? Now, you might be inclined to think that MPs who draw big pensions for life after six years in the House of Commons are a SIG, too. But you'd be wrong. They're not. I'm not quite sure why they're not, but I expect I'll figure it out eventually.

11 Suffer the Little Children

> Our patriarchal society has set the conditions for sexual assaults and harassment, including the sexual abuse of children...such behaviour has for too long been tolerated in our society...one of the most significant tasks ahead of us is to make major changes in the underlying deeply rooted attitudes of sexism.
> Rix G. Rogers, Special Advisor on
> Child Sexual Abuse to the Minister of Health
> and Welfare, 1990

MOUNT CASHEL

There were very few dry eyes among those of us who followed the Hughes Inquiry. You could be sitting there watching a young man speaking into a microphone, and suddenly you could see the little boy of seven or ten or fourteen, in the orphanage, frightened, confused, not knowing where to turn. "If only we had known," we kept thinking. "If only we could have done something to help..." And most of us, I think, wished there was some way we could communicate to those witnesses our respect and gratitude for the courage they showed in telling their stories again.

That is one of the important things that the media coverage of this inquiry did: it gave us a small insight into how difficult it can be for victims of child abuse to come forward to relive experiences they so much want to forget. With the Hughes Inquiry, the ordeal of the Mount Cashel boys was still not over. They would still have to face questioning by the lawyers for the accused, a cross-examination intended to diminish their credibility.

It can be a lonely and painful struggle for those who speak out. These are things that crown prosecutors, social workers, and the staff of transition houses have known for a very long time. Some years ago, one of these professionals told of a nine-year-old girl who was finally brave enough to confide in her teacher that her father was hurting her. She had suffered sexual abuse from him since she was an infant. After her father was charged, she had to endure the ordeal of the courtroom. Then, when he was sentenced to jail, her mother and brother turned on her for bringing disgrace on the family, for sending Daddy to jail.

It is no wonder that the victims of such crimes have so often kept their anguish to themselves and suffered alone. And that's what the abusers have counted on.

But what we have been learning lately is that when one victim finds the courage to speak out, it gives others the courage to do the same. The two little girls whose first faltering complaints brought the case of a United Church minister and doctor to light some years ago had cried into their pillows for many a night, confused and fearful, until a public service announcement on television told them that no one had the right to do sexual things to them. That advertisement made it possible for them to tell their mother, in spite of the warnings and threats the family doctor had made to them.

So to the young men of Mount Cashel, and to all the girls and boys and women and men who have spoken out about the abuse they have suffered, and to those who have helped them and gone to their defence, we owe not only our admiration and respect. We also owe them our gratitude. By exposing the dark secrets that our society has allowed to fester behind closed doors, they have empowered others and made it more difficult for such outrages to be repeated.

That is why an ad hoc committee of social action and women's groups organized a special public gathering to say to them, "THANK YOU FOR YOUR COURAGE." We believed that most people wanted to express their gratitude, but felt powerless to do it individually, so we have planned an occasion where we could do it together. It took place, appropriately, on Thanksgiving Day, 1989, in Bannerman Park.

It was a simple event. There was a short walk around the neighbourhood, then a return to the park for a brief address by vocalist Anita Best, and a bit of singing. And as a lasting reminder, we planted crocuses—crocuses for courage.

And each spring, those brave little flowers poking up through the snow will remind us of the quiet heroism of the people who are helping to make the ugly secret of child abuse a thing of the past.

THE BOYS FROM ST. VINCENT.

There has been much discussion of the film, *The Boys From St. Vincent* since it was first shown on CBC in the fall of 1993. Seldom have I heard such universal praise for a dramatic production. People were grateful that the film told the story honestly and without exploitation.

The pain and fear of the children was unforgettable. The adults who participated in the cover-up were unforgettable, too, and one of the more repulsive elements in the film. It is a film where the characters in fiction refer us back to fact. Do the real perpetrators sleep at night, one wonders? Did it never bother them? How can it be that those in power chose to protect the institution rather than the child? How could they use their positions to crucify children?

There were precious few heroes in the story. Apart from some honest cops, the hero in this fictionalized film, as in the real Mount Cashel story, was the handyman and janitor. Phil Dinn was wonderfully cast in the role and warmed our hearts with his blunt and rough-edged decency.

In the early days of raising public awareness around this issue, the CBC received a lot of criticism for daring to tell the humiliating details of sexual abuse of children by the medical doctor/United Church minister and by a well-known and highly popular priest.

The public wasn't used to hearing such grim stories about respected public figures, and the fact that such important men were brought before the courts came as a shock. Usually, influential offenders were whisked away to warmer climates. Unforgivably, some even turned on the victims for daring to tell the truth about their abuse at the hands of important men. People didn't want to believe what they were hearing.

Sexual assaults weren't taken all that seriously. Some believed that, once the painful event of rape was over, the incident could be forgotten. Even the courts were unaware of how long-lasting and devastating are the effects. That has changed, but only because we have begun to listen to the survivors and because agencies have sponsored special awareness sessions for police and the judiciary. There is no excuse today for ignorance.

It is worth remembering that if the publicity surrounding the case of the abusive priest had not been so widespread, we might never have learned the truth about Mount Cashel.

Shane Earle might not have found the courage to try once again to be heard had he not finally witnessed a powerful man being brought to justice. It was Shane who blew the case wide open. And it's the combination of all those factors that led to the Hughes Commission and the consequent court cases.

And, in turn, it was the young men of Mount Cashel who freed others who had been abused in orphanages and native residential schools and juvenile detention centres and foster homes in provinces and territories all across Canada, to come forward with their stories.

The story of child abuse is far from finished yet, though. It comes in many forms, and one that we have barely begun to tackle is the hidden problem of incest.

Years ago, I was speaking to a PTA group about violence and the effects on children and on women. At tea-time a woman in her eighties took me outside into the hall where we could be alone. She took my hands, and hers were trembling as she said, "You know what you were saying in there about incest? That happened to me when I was five and continued until I could leave home." Her father had died when she was in her thirties, and she had been glad. There was never a day in her life when she didn't relive the horror of what he had done to her.

Later I spoke to a clergyman in attendance. "I understand incest is a problem in this community," I said. "Oh yes," he said. "There's a family just down the road, and another across the street and...." It sounded like the odd case of mumps or measles.

There are always mixed feelings about whether sordid stories of sexual abuse should be publicized. My columns on the subject provoked a former resident of Mount Cashel to write that he had not been abused in the orphanage but he said, "I feel I am being abused by people like you."

His hurt was understandable. He had been lucky, and resented the embarrassment. I was not unmoved by his words but found agreement with another reader who strengthened my resolve:

> As one who is not entirely uninformed about sexual abuse I write to commend you for your article in today's Telegram which I read with interest and satisfaction. I am convinced that the only defence against this nefarious conduct, which is endemic in mankind, is exposure and in constant reminders that it will not be tolerated. My concern is that because it is nasty, high levels of government do not like dealing with it as it is politically explosive, the churches do not want to be involved for obvious reasons and

many friends and acquaintances of mine, and I gather some of yours, do not want to read, see or hear about it because it depresses them.

All of this, it seems to me is a recipe for sweeping the whole issue back again under the carpet where it was hidden for so long...Keep up your good work.

1-800-668-6868

When a special toll-free telephone number was established as a children's crisis line that kids in trouble anywhere in Canada could call for help and advice, it seemed like a great idea. I hadn't seen the number advertised much, apart from catching an occasional announcement on television, but I assumed that it was well publicized in schools, churches, community centres, children's hospitals, youth clubs, and wherever children were.

But listening to the Hughes Inquiry with its vivid demonstrations of how important it is that children have somewhere to turn for help, I started to think more about the crisis line. Would a child in trouble be likely to know the number? Could she or he find it out easily? I knew there was such a number, but I didn't know what it was. Suppose I were a child being abused at home or at school. How would I find out where to call?

So I called Information (411) and asked, "Can you tell me the toll-free crisis number that children can call if they need help?" The operator thought about that for a while, then said, "Crisis number? For children? Never heard of it. Just a moment, please." After a considerable pause she came back on the line: "Here it is. Toll-free. 1-800-661-9960." I was pretty sure that was not right, but I tried it. A recording told me that my call could not be completed as dialled.

So I tried Long Distance Information for toll-free numbers, 1-800-555-1212. I put my question, and a pleasant young male voice answered: "Can you tell me the name of the association?" I explained that I wasn't looking for an association. This was an emergency number that children could call for help. "What is your area code?" he asked. I couldn't see what that had to do with anything, but I gave it to him. "I have something called the Children's Foundation listed in Toronto," he told me finally. I told him I didn't think that was it.

Hmmm. Well, it's government sponsored, right? Let's look at the blue pages. Under Frequently Called Numbers I found an entry for Child Abuse Treatment and Prevention. Sounded promising. The answer there:

"I don't know... A child could certainly call here... The supervisor might know, but she's on another line."

I was beginning to take the whole thing more seriously now. What if I really were a child who needed help and had finally worked up the courage to try and find it? People with titles like "supervisor" can be pretty intimidating for a troubled youngster. This was supposed to be a special kind of line with people who know how to talk to kids. I decided not to wait.

How about the Janeway Children's Hospital? A child who had received treatment there might think of it as a place to ask for the number. I called and recited my question again. "Children in trouble?" was the response. "What kind of trouble?" I suggested a child being abused by adults. "Yes, we have that number," I was told. "Just a minute." There was a long pause and a background noise of several voices, and then the original voice returned to give me a telephone number. "But that doesn't begin with 800. It's not a toll-free number," I said. "Oh, well," came the reply, "you'll have to ask them about that."

So I dialled 911 for emergency calls. "We have no listing," they said. "Perhaps the police could tell you."

A real child in trouble, of course, might not want to talk to police: that's one of the reasons for setting up a crisis line in the first place. However, I dialled 722-5111. The first person I spoke to said, "Just a minute, please." After a short pause, another voice came on the line: "I'm not really sure. There's a place on LeMarchant where kids can just walk in... Just a minute, I'll transfer you to headquarters."

Headquarters: "No, I don't know the number...but you could try information... (pause)...I have a number here for suicide prevention...(pause)...But wait just a minute until I ask somebody else." There was a longer pause and then, finally, the right answer: "1-800-668-6868."

There was one call left to make: the crisis line itself. Perhaps I could tell them of the difficulty I had getting the right number. The phone rang and was answered promptly—by a recording: "KID'S HELP. PLEASE HOLD...THE LINES ARE BUSY..."

I was thinking that if I were a little girl suffering abuse from an incestuous father or a little boy being cruelly treated in a foster home, I wouldn't know where to go for help today any more than I would have in the past. Having the line is a step in the right direction: now, why couldn't we see that everybody knows it? In fact, why have a number at all? Why can't the telephone company tell kids just to phone "O" and be connected? Or, if we do have a number, why can't it spell KIDS or HELP or something easy?

Maybe it should be advertised on milk cartons or pop cans. Surely any responsible company would want to cooperate. In the meantime, do the teachers at your school know the number? Does your church? Or doctor? Why not check around a bit?

Now this is all based on the assumption that when a child is able to get through to the line, it actually works. That too might need checking out. It does seem today that there has been much more publicity about the Help Line. Unfortunately there is probably even more need for it.

BELIEVE THE CHILD

"Suffer the little children and forbid them not to come unto me; for of such is the kingdom of heaven" (Matthew 19:14). Those lines are heard from many a pulpit during the Christmas season. But how do we, as a society, really behave?

Rix Rogers, a special adviser to a federal health minister, said:

> Although Canadians like to think of themselves as a kindly, child-loving people, the facts do not bear out this rosy image. A truer picture is that Canadians give lip service to valuing their children, while leaving them at the mercy of a cold, purely adult-oriented society... The basic source of protection for children—the family—is too often a source of abuse and stress instead. And the recourse from an abusive family—the legal system—is capable of victimizing the child all over again through insensitive handling (*Toronto Star*, Jan. 13, 1989).

An editorial in the *Globe and Mail* (Dec. 14, 1989) stated:

> One frustrating feature of poverty in a country such as Canada is its invisibility. Ours is not the Ethiopian poverty of the swollen belly or sunken-eyed dehydration. It is, rather, of the type that makes a thousand subtle subtractions from the bodies and minds of people in its grip, draining them of health, hope and opportunity... More than a million children suffer from poverty in Canada.

There are 52 food banks in Newfoundland, 22 of them in St. John's. There are more food banks in Toronto than there are McDonald's restaurants. Children make up one fourth of food bank recipients. At the same time, Toronto retailers note that Mercedes Benzes, Porsches, Cadillacs and other luxury cars have been selling in record numbers.

In Winnipeg, seven-year-old girls sell sex in a prostitution ring, according to the executive director of a children's home in that city. In Toronto, police warn of pimps who recruit young girls, "We've had a girl with multiple sclerosis—she walks with two canes—and she's picked up (by a pimp) instantly," said a constable with the Metro police force.

In St. John's, a defendant in a case of incest argues to the judge that he broke in her mother, why shouldn't he break in his daughter too? A judge in Stephenville gives a man two weeks in jail for impaired driving, and a suspended sentence for a man convicted of child abuse.

In Vancouver, a judge describes a three-year old victim in a sex abuse case as "sexually aggressive." A caller on a St. John's open-line show calls all little girls "vamps."

A Kids Help phone line barely manages to get temporary funding from the federal government. Meanwhile, 38 strip bars are funded through a federal government agency to the tune of 17 million dollars.

A St. John's radio station urges its mostly young audience to buy mistletoe belt buckles for Christmas, demeaning human relationships and Christmas in the interests of commerce.

Store owners uncaringly sell war toys to children, and some parents continue to put guns and tanks under the Christmas tree for their sons to play with. Adults make garish "Garbage Pail Kids" cards full of violence and contempt for human values, and other adults sell them to children. A magazine called "Slaughterhouse" joins the gory detective magazines in the newsstands, from which children can learn how entertaining it is to watch scenes of violence and sadism that would have shocked the torturers at the Spanish Inquisition.

Somehow, I don't think that kind of suffering of little children was what Jesus had in mind.

At a seminar sponsored by the Roman Catholic School Board, counsellor Beth Allan told the audience that the most damaging thing that can happen to a child is to not be believed when he or she finally finds the courage to tell someone their story of abuse. And child specialist Dan Wiseman begged members of the audience to remember only one thing from his address: to "believe the child." He said that research had shown that children, on average, had to tell their story eight times before anyone would believe them. And, he added, most children give up after the first telling.

Just a few years ago, Canada signed the United Nations Convention on the Rights of the Child. It's up to us whether that is allowed to remain a token gesture or whether it will have tangible results. Like charity, children's rights begin at home.

12 Whose Country is it Anyway?

God bless the poor for they don't have you to look after them.
Mary Jane Connolly Greer

These were my mother's last words to my sister. As a nurse and minister's wife she never forgot the rank poverty she saw in Canada before the introduction of medicare and social programs.

UNIVERSALITY

Prime Minister Louis St. Laurent was the first person in Canada to receive the Old Age Pension in 1951. He made a big splash about it to illustrate the fact that the pension belonged to every Canadian citizen over the age of 70—that it was a pension paid to *all* seniors. There was no stigma attached: rich or poor, everybody in that age group would simply receive $40 in the mail every month.

It was another universal program, similar in purpose to the Family Allowance introduced in 1944. It came at a time when people were determined to get away from humiliating "relief" programs that were long on red tape and short on assistance, and to do away with the hated "means test" that forced needy people to suffer all sorts of humiliation.

In the late 1950s, as a social worker, I had a client whose sense of pride and independence was so strong that she was unable to fill out the simple form required for the Old Age Pension. She had been raised in a time when "relief" marked desperate recipients as lazy and shiftless, and applicants were made to grovel before receiving it.

Her life had been a bitter struggle. As a young bride she had accompanied her coal miner husband from Scotland to a small mining town in British Columbia where they sought to make a better life. Miners were paid almost nothing before they organized into a union. Bitter strikes had to take place, causing desperate misery before they were able to win certification. And even after they won the right to be unionized, the wages were inadequate for the work they performed. Safety precautions were minimal, lives were cheap and there was no security for workers or their families.

This tall, proud woman had brought her stern views of Christian morality with her from her home in Glasgow. She had been a lifelong believer in hard work, in cleanliness being next to godliness, and in personal duty to overcome (or put up with) misfortune. But it had not saved her from the misery of poverty in old age.

I had received notice that she was eligible for the pension and had gone to interview her and see whether she needed assistance to fill out the papers to qualify. But she couldn't do it. She beat around the bush. She said she would die rather than accept charity. She was just fine, had no financial problems. How dare I assume she needed help?

I knew how much she needed that small pension, so I kept making repeated visits to her house. She would talk about the past, sometimes say a prayer or two and do anything but look at the forms I had laid on the table. I would talk about how much we owe the people who built our country, how the pension was just one small way in which Canada gave something back to the pioneers. I argued this had nothing to do with charity. Sure, the Prime Minister himself received it!

Her husband had been killed in the coal mine. There was no pension for widows. Her three tall sons in their forties had spent their lives working in the mines, but coal was being replaced by oil and the work was becoming sporadic. Three of the five mines in her town had closed permanently, and the remaining two were working short shifts. The mother felt she was a burden to her sons who had their own responsibilities.

She came close every so often to signing, but her pride held her back. She felt so deeply the stigma and shame of being poor, as though she was responsible for her plight.

One day I came into her kitchen and said "Look, I've filled in all the information. They only thing left for you to do is to put your signature on the bottom, then I won't bother you anymore. Think how free you'll be without me having tea in your kitchen once a week."

She didn't answer directly. "My sons told me you were down in the mine the other day," she said. That was true. A man who later would turn out to be my husband had organized a bunch of teachers and invited us social workers and public health nurses to go with them on a tour of the mine. What it is to be young and fearless! I can't imagine now how I put on the helmet with the light, and went down the shaft into the bowels of the earth just like a miner would.

Anyway, my Scottish lady liked the fact that I had gone into the mine. I don't know if that's what tipped the balance, or whether she was just sick and tired of seeing me, but she signed. She asked me if I was married—because, she said, she didn't approve of married women working. As I wasn't, she gave me two precious jars of her raspberry jam. I have never forgotten her and the thousands more she represented, from the widows in St. Lawrence, Newfoundland or, God help them, the miners and their families in Nova Scotia and in the Northwest Territories.

I tell her story now as a way of ringing an alarm bell that should be rung across the country. While our collective attention was occupied poring over constitutional headaches, the Mulroney government ended the first universal program in Canada, the Family Allowance. And we shouldn't have let it happen. It was done under the pious pretence that the government would now be directing the funds to the people who really need it instead of giving it to the higher income people who don't need it. As if they cared.

We fought that battle nearly fifty years ago. One of the main points of universal schemes was that they saved the trouble and enormous expense of administering humiliating programs that had to determine who was and who wasn't eligible. Those who didn't need the allowance would be giving it back in their income tax. Even more important, it prevented people in need from being stripped of their dignity by prying inspectors.

If money paid out in universal programs is not coming back in taxes from people who don't need it, the solution is not to do away with the universal program, but to overhaul the income tax system.

We must protect our remaining universal programs. Before the 1993 election, the Liberals issued a Red Book full of promises similar to Mulroney's that guaranteed a total commitment to social programs. After election, also like Mulroney, they began work dismantling them.

MADNESS OR TREASON

Remember *The Caine Mutiny*? Humphrey Bogart as Captain Queeg goes madder and madder, feverishly rattling a pair of ball-bearings in his hand, alternating between wild irrationality and a kind of crafty persuasiveness, putting the ship in greater and greater danger. Everyone is terrified, but he is the Captain. Nobody knows what to do.

If that doesn't sound familiar to Canadians, it should. For eight years, we had a man on the bridge in Ottawa who rattled his dice and issued smarmy platitudes about responsibility while slashing at every cherished social commitment and institution that we have fought for and developed over the years. The ship was headed for the rocks, and on the lower deck we were getting more and more frightened, but the officers seemed helpless and impotent.

During the Mulroney era, hardly a week went by without a fresh assault on another sacred trust. The lower the government sank in opinion polls, the more manic the Prime Minister became about destroying Canada. Each attack created a trickle-down effect that Canadians were getting all too used to.

When we lost the railway and ferries were reduced, airports cut back, post offices slaughtered, unemployment insurance chopped, regional disparity grants curtailed, it wasn't just employees or recipients who suffered or communities that went under, tragic as that is. Stores and services went under, too, and the effect keeps spiralling.

The cuts to the CBC threatened to kill something else too: a vision of a country that took years to develop. A Canadian commitment that our communication system would justly represent all regions across the country equally and authentically from their own place.

It's a view of how much you love this wild, sprawling nation by respecting the integrity of each part. It's a view of unity that recognizes we can only be united if we know each other and have a chance to cement bonds of respect and friendship.

Any nation proud of its heritage has a national communication system that reflects its people. It's why the dreamers and supporters of the CBC have always pushed for a mandate that emphasized local and regional programming. No other country in the world would let its leaders destroy its national culture, and we can't afford to either.

Of course, there was more to come. Captain Queeg was after our medicare system, too. The intention of Bill 69 was to dismantle the medical care system, piece by piece, until we found ourselves back to the days when only the rich were entitled to proper medical care. I don't know of any issue that should propel people out into the streets more than this one. Younger people don't know what it was like to live in a country without medicare, and maybe some older ones have forgotten. But we forget at our peril.

When I was practising social work in a small mining town on Vancouver Island, one of my client families was headed by a man who was chronically ill with silicosis. In those days the worker's compensation board wouldn't recognize this as a disease caused by working in coal mines. The law finally changed but only after the wife of another miner sat for months, every single day, on the steps of the B.C. Legislature to demand her husband's rights. But that came later. My client had no compensation.

He was tall and gaunt and very ill. He couldn't work. His wife had died, leaving him to care for six children. One daughter, after a bout of rheumatic fever, spent most of her days on the settle in the kitchen suffering from a heart condition. None of the family ever went near a doctor if they could help it because they couldn't afford to.

What broke my heart was that this proud man, looking after his children so caringly, had to fork out $6.00 every month (which would be like $60 today) from his welfare cheque to pay the outstanding medical bills—bills run up years earlier during his wife's terminal illness and his daughter's struggle with rheumatic fever. There were lots of times he went hungry in order to pay the doctor's bill.

There's nothing unique in that story. It's a familiar tale all across Canada for anyone who remembers what it was like to be without medicare. But, by God, it's worth remembering right now.

In the Caine Mutiny, the officers knew their captain was mad and they knew their ship was in danger of going under, but they were afraid to act because the age-old law of the sea defined any contravention of the captain's orders as mutiny, a capital offence.

The members of the Mulroney cabinet and the PC caucus were bound by no such law. They didn't even have to step up on the bridge and clap the captain in irons. Any of them who had the good of Canada at heart—who valued their country more than they valued their political perks and patronage—had only to withdraw their support.

They didn't have to join the Liberals or the NDP or the Bloc Québecois or the Reform Party. All they had to do was take away their votes to prevent their mad captain from sinking us all. And they should have. Anything else is madness. Or treason. It still seems strange to me that out of the massive Tory caucus there wasn't one member who defected.

Fortunately, a country is not a ship, and we were able to hand the Mulroney/Campbell Tories the most stunning defeat in history.

The nice, folksy, down-home captain who took over the bridge didn't rattle dice or ball-bearings, but he carried right on with the same sort of policies. So, if it isn't madness...

CORPORATE GREED

In 1993, I wrote a column called "Mummy, What's a Post Office?" I got an interesting response from Marilyn Farley, Communications Manager for the Atlantic Division of Canada Post (*Evening Telegram*, March 6, 1993).

Come to think of it, I'm not sure it should be called a reply, since she did not really deal with the things I was complaining about—such as the closure of post offices and the deficiencies in service.

Mainly, she seemed to be concerned with pointing out what a great job Canada Post was doing at becoming a business. "We must remain progressive and competitive," she said, "so that we will never again have to depend on Canadian taxpayers to keep us afloat." In my view, that is a bit like the Department of Highways becoming a profit-making enterprise, but let us have a look at the points she covered.

First, "progressive." It used to be that when a new subdivision opened up, the householders got an address and mail delivery simultaneously. In rural areas, it used to be that people could pick up their mail, buy a few stamps, pass the time of day with a neighbour or two, and catch up on the gossip from the postmistress or postmaster, as the case might be. I do not regard the substitution of windswept green boxes drifted in with snow as progress. St. John's is down to one and a half genuine post offices, and I don't regard that as progress, either.

Then, "competitive." But with whom? And doing what? There are a lot of courier services out there, but is anybody trying to compete with Canada Post at what we really want a national postal service to do—delivering our mail in the most comfortable, efficient, and convenient manner possible? Ms. Farley proudly announced that Canada Post "maintains the largest collection and delivery service in Canada." Well, isn't that what most people would expect a country's postal service to do?

And how about not depending on taxpayers to keep afloat? As far as I can see, it is taxpayers who have been losing services, losing jobs in their communities, and losing cash to meet regular increases in rates or to use alternate services.

From 1986 to 1993, Canada Post laid off 3,000 people from rural post office jobs, 83% of them women.

One owner of a small business in St. John's decided to sue Canada Post for breaking its own regulations by closing Station A to small business. His claim was based on the fact that impeding or slowing down the mail is an illegal act. Closing the box he had been renting for twenty years and moving his import business to a totally inadequate drug store location certainly impeded his mail, slowed down his access to it and would prove costly to his business.

I heard from a number of people who were angered by Ms. Farley's reply. One woman phoned from Burin to say that both she and her husband had called her to put the record straight. She told of sending a letter that cost $3.25 for postage and took 13 days to reach its destination. A parcel costing $14 took nine days. We mailed a small parcel and were told that it would cost $3.50 to arrive in 11 working days or we could pay $8.75 for preferred delivery.

Meanwhile, Canada Post was in the process of constructing a ninety-million-dollar "postal palace" in Ottawa. Apparently our provincial post offices would not have died in vain. There would be a suitable monument in the capital city. Mainly, it would house executive offices.

At the time of Ms. Farley's letter, Canada Post's Chief Executive Officer, Donald Landers, appointed by the Prime Minister, was paying himself $250,000 a year. Performance bonuses of 25%, would bring his annual income to $312,000. Other perks included a chauffeur-driven limousine, first-class air travel and lavish pension benefits. He was awarded the Order of Canada.

Since taking over in 1986, Mr. Landers saw to it that over 1300 rural post offices were closed or privatized. The 3,800 or so remaining ones were threatened as well. At the same time, he doubled the executive force to include 70 senior executives who would work in the new building in Ottawa at salaries ranging from $150,000 to $250,000. Along with these "competitive" salaries, go "performance bonuses," cars, generous pensions, expenses on the corporate credit card, and free tickets to professional sports events. Canada Post has private boxes at the Skydome in Toronto (leased at $250,000 a year) and the Northlands Coliseum in Edmonton (leased at $300,000 a year).

Postal rates were raised to meet these high living expenditures, and from 1986 to 1993 the revenue increased from one billion to four billion. Rather than apply it to wipe out the postal deficit, this added revenue strangely disappeared into other things.

In other western countries, the U.S., Britain and Australia, a large portion of the mail is delivered the next day. Canada's standards are the worst in the western world. And for that you're awarded the Order of Canada and housed in a multi-million-dollar building.

Ms. Farley enthusiastically defended these changes as being similar to those of other businesses preparing for the twenty-first century. Of course, in that she was absolutely correct. This was the corporate agenda for Canada that the Tory government promised with more and more unemployed, communities under-serviced, and the boys at the top given perks from our pocketbooks that can only be described as obscene.

Ms. Farley called it progress. I call it callous corporate greed.

13 War and Women

Often women who work in the peace and ecological movements for true disarmament and for a demilitarized society are portrayed (misleadingly so) as expressing their so-called true nature, since women are said to be the guardians of life on earth. But we are working in these movements, *not* because we are meek or weak. We work in these movements because we have become very angry, angry on our own behalf, angry for our sisters, angry on behalf of our children and the entire planet earth...

We invite all men who oppose violence to join us in our cause for peace. We urge them to break out of their *rigid* patriarchal institutions and out of their own conditioning!
Petra Kelly, The Green Party,
Federal Republic of Germany

THE BORDELLO CAMPS OF BOSNIA

One day in 1993, a man from Mount Pearl phoned me about a column I had written on the rape and murder of Bosnian women. He expressed his horror that soldiers could be ordered by their commanding officers to go out and rape women. He added that no command in the world could make him commit such atrocity. He couldn't understand how any man could, no matter who gave the command. His stomach turned with revulsion as he read the accounts of the tortured women and of the Serbian goal of ethnic cleansing in that God-awful war. And he protested that he couldn't understand why the world isn't standing together in universal condemnation and offering help to the victims.

A woman wrote to say how glad she was that I had raised the issue: "I find it appalling that even though there have been sporadic reports in the newspapers and on CBC about the sanctioned rape of Bosnian women, there has been no outcry of protest or any suggestion of investigation from any government. It makes one feel very helpless. Your article expressed the outrage I was feeling..."

After receiving those remarks, I also received a number of documents compiled by the women's movement in Bosnia-Herzegovina. Reading their stories and testimonials took me back to the days in which we were learning the horror of what had happened to Jews in those never-to-be-forgotten Nazi concentration camps. We thought the world would never again allow such unbearable things to happen to human beings. But the war in Sarajevo was as monstrously evil as any war before it. And my respondents were right; we must demand action to help the women and children trapped in today's concentration camps.

The material sent to the Canadian women's movement came from several women's groups, "Tresnjevika" in Zagreb, Mothers for Peace in Croatia, the Zagreb Women's Lobby, women working in the "Autonomous Women's House," and Kareta feminist group and publication (the first post-World War Two feminist journal in Yugoslavia). They appealed to world opinion to help them in demanding that the rape-death camps be closed immediately. They claimed that "the topic of sexual abuse is still treated as a secondary concern within the world organizations and the media which are investigating the war crimes that are occurring on these territories."

The women wrote, "The existence of rape-death camps must be understood as a strategy or fact of genocide, of a `final solution.' Unlike rape camps which were set up during the wars in, for example, Vietnam, Afghanistan and Korea, the camps in Bosnia-Herzegovina and Croatia are not solely sexual abuse centres but are a part of an organized system leading to liquidation, i.e. ethnic cleansing of Muslim and Croatian nationalities. Sexual abuses in this context have modern precedents only in Nazi Germany."

Sixteen rape-death camps were listed in Bosnia-Herzegovina: several hotels, a motel, a restaurant, a secondary school, mountain locations, villages and towns that were scenes of past massacres. They were camps where soldiers came repeatedly to gang-rape the women and often to murder them as well.

In Sarajevo, not far from the Holiday Inn, where media organizations were staying, bodies of raped and murdered women and girls were found in basements. The youngest was an eight-year-old girl who was raped before her throat was cut. One victim was beheaded.

A women's prison located outside of Bosnia at a train station held 814 Muslim prisoners. At the motel in Vilina Vlas, 200 young girls from eastern Bosnia were in prison for four months. "Serb soldiers would return from the front to the motels and rape the girls. While raping them they would tell stories of how they killed people in the surrounding Muslim villages and that they should be happy that Serbs are impregnating them and that they will bear Serbian children. Many of these girls became pregnant. Of the 200 girls, five committed suicide, six escaped and the others were killed."

The material contained personal accounts that I felt I could not reprint. But I was torn by the dilemma that if we don't know what happened, we prolong suffering by not doing anything. Since reading their accounts I can't get the pictures of those desperate people out of my mind; the mother who screamed the whole time her young daughter was being raped. The father who was forced to watch the gang-rape of his 12-year-old child. The 10-year-old boy forced to witness his mother's rape. The girl who cried, "I can't repeat the horror I lived through anymore...not even the most diabolic mind can imagine this...the Second World War looks like a fairy tale compared to this war...Why is the world not doing anything? ...Isn't it enough that we've lived through this?...there are more concentration camps and thousands of women and girls whom they torture."

Is it because rape has always been considered a natural spoil of war that the full horror of what was happening to the women and children in Bosnia was not being taken as seriously as it demanded? Or is it because world leaders are mainly men who have not shared the revulsion experienced by the reader who phoned me?

In Canada, we still hear from judges who claim, as one did in recent years in Nova Scotia, that the rape "without violence" of a 14-year-old girl was not serious enough to warrant a jail sentence.

Figures from Bosnia-Herzegovina indicate that over 50,000 women and children endured the most frightful methods of terror and torture.

The Women's Group,"Tresnjevika," demanded that the bordello camps be shut down immediately. And that women's rights to sexual and reproductive control be upheld absolutely and without compromise. And they asked, "To this end of condemning and halting the war crimes, we appeal to all international organizations and to all women's groups to assist us."

What was our government doing? Does anybody care about the rape/death camps of women?

LEST WE FORGET

Another Armistice Day, the day we set aside to remember the horrors of war, has come and gone. The sad thing is that each new one brings us fresh horrors to remember. It will be a long time before we forget the heartbroken voice of the man from Enniskillen telling of how he held his dying daughter's hand as they both lay buried in the rubble left by a terrorist bomb. That ghastly event will take its place beside all the others, reaching back from our own time to that of our parents and grandparents: Nicaragua, Vietnam, Sharpeville, Korea, Dieppe, Beaumont-Hamel—the list goes on and on.

My own personal memories go back farther than many, I suppose, to the days leading up to the Second World War.

I was a child in Vancouver in that time of the Great Depression when hordes of young men rode the freight trains westward from the cold prairies in search of work—or at least a warmer climate. Then the war came along. And suddenly there was full employment: jobs for everyone, including women, who were not merely encouraged to put their children into the ample daycare that was provided, they were told that it would be downright disloyal not to. The same young unemployed men who had been called lazy and shiftless—and told to go west—sound familiar?—because they were unable to find work suddenly became heroes in uniform, cheered and applauded as they headed out to kill other young men for King and Country.

But my "forever" memory centres on my older brother who, a telegram informed us in 1943, was listed as missing after his Lancaster bomber was shot down in an air raid over Germany. We learned six weeks later that he was alive and in a prisoner of war camp. He survived it, and after he returned home told us of the painful forced marches that took place in the closing days of the war, as prisoners were moved ahead of the advancing Allied forces.

There was very little food. The prisoners would knock on the doors of German farmhouses as they passed, asking for something to eat in a few halting German phrases, and often the farmers would give what they could. The German guards were no better off than the prisoners, and what little food there was they shared.

Cliff came home, not hating the Germans as we were trained to do by the propaganda mills, but hating a system that pitted the citizens of one country against the citizens of another.

It was a German mother who bathed his wounds and torn face after his plane was shot down and his parachute landed in her field. She wept for him as the German soldiers came to take him away. Neither she nor her husband wanted to turn him over to the authorities, but what else could they do?

It wasn't the ordinary people in Germany who started the war. Hitler had many allies in the people who made their millions out of the armament industry, and many of them came from the nations who later commanded the youth of their countries to go out and fight against an enemy they had supplied with weapons.

Cliff went to university after he came home, as did many young men and women. He took part in parliamentary forums at the University of British Columbia, where he argued and debated for a system of democratic government that would find a way to put an end to war. He started, with others, a student exchange program with German students in an effort to bring healing between the two nations. In the process he met another young student as concerned as he was to find the ways that would lead to a peaceful future. His new friend was Helmut Schmidt, who went on to become the Chancellor of West Germany.

They both believed that the hope of the world lay in ordinary citizens being the voice of government, rather than the wealthy and the powerful. They saw the intermingling of students and other citizens from countries around the world as the hope for the future, and to that end put great faith in the developing forum of the United Nations.

That organization, although it has plenty of faults, has been instrumental in lessening world tensions and looking for peaceful resolution. We would certainly have been the losers in a world that lacked the tremendous influence of the United Nations Assembly.

So I, like most of us, have no trouble remembering what November 11 represents. It's what I think of when I march in the peace parade in Stephenville or downtown in St. John's. It's the reason I applaud heartily the work of the fine young people in the Ploughshares Youth organization. It's why I was present in spirit, at least, one weekend in Corner Brook at the absolutely splendid peace conference they held in their city. It's why I support the work of Voice of Women and am proud that in every large or small women's rights group, the commitment to peace is at the top of every agenda.

If we really care about the sacrifices made in two world wars we need to be doing everything in our power to teach children non-violence and the ethics of peace. We must counteract the messages that are coming at them in song, in movies and on television and even in toys that all condone and glorify the use of violence.

A reader sent me a brochure that is indicative of the kind of sick messages that are being peddled to children. It filled her with revulsion. The ad is for a train set "that will turn your friends green with envy," the brochure says. It is huge and can be made even bigger by putting two together into a "super-system." But here's the real clincher: "you can even stage your own crashes and catastrophes...imagine the excitement of two trains hurtling towards each other full steam ahead—and coming together in a spectacular collision that flings them violently from the tracks." What makes it even more grotesque is that this toy and this message are being sold as a Christmas present for children.

If we really want to remember what Armistice Day means, we need to condemn mightily the television programs and the toy and clothing manufacturers who push their violent messages on the young as though killing is the symbol for Christmas.

Lest we forget.

14 A Planet Worth Saving

The values of technology have so permeated the public mind that all too frequently what is efficient is seen as the right thing to do.
    Dr. Ursula Franklin, Physicist.

THE TALE OF THE BLUE HERON

Two trees near our house have had pieces of plastic bags caught in them for the last three years. Through all the storms, ice attacks, high winds and the occasional solar heat, they have been constant reminders of the longevity of polluting materials. Nothing, it seems, can tear them loose. Not only are they ugly; now I know plastic bags can be dangerous too. I've become a bit of a fanatic about it, chasing after them when I'm outdoors, tying them in knots and depositing them in containers where they can't escape.

This fanaticism all started with a phone call from our second son. He had been mowing the lawn in front of his house in Vancouver when a neighbour tapped him on the arm to shut off the machine, pointing to the roof. There, perched on the peak, was a big blue heron with a plastic bag over its head.

Son Number Two was always finding animals in distress when he was small, and he has not changed all that much. He was not about to abandon the heron, even though it probably posed the greatest animal rescue challenge of his career. Prudently, he first called the SPCA. They were sympathetic, but could not help. They said that by the time they could get anybody there, the bird would be gone. He was on his own.

The first thing was to find a long pole and add a hook made from a coat hanger so that he might be able to pull the bag loose if the bird would let him get that close. The second thing to do was to get up to where the heron was. These things accomplished, he edged along the roof peak quietly, pole in hand, coming closer and closer. Of course, just as he extended the pole the heron launched itself blindly into the air and flew erratically off over the neighbouring housetops.

Standing on the roof SuperSon thought he saw where she had blindly blundered into some trees and come to rest. He made his way down as fast as he could, and he and the neighbour set off in pursuit, Son on foot, Neighbour on bicycle.

They chased down lanes, crawled behind hedges and up on garages. Along the way, their antics attracted the attention of a man working on a backhoe. When he learned what was happening, he promptly joined the search, with his backhoe.

They finally located their quarry and made another cautious approach into someone's yard. The heron flapped over the fence and landed into another neighbour's garden. SuperSon tore around to the front to enter by the gate, and inside found the heron being eyed terrifyingly by a humungous dog.

The animal could not decide which of the two strange creatures to attack first, so it roared at them both, allowing time for each of them to take off over different fences, both flying.

This time, the heron headed in the direction of a nearby park but, in her non-seeing panic, flew right into a tree and dropped to the ground. The would-be rescuers descended, full of concern, but just as they reached her she revived and took off again back in the direction they had just come.

So the strange parade started off down the laneways again. Families peacefully barbecuing in their back gardens were treated to the sight of a man on a bicycle apparently being pursued by a perspiring man on foot, who was apparently being pursued by a man on a big yellow backhoe. They ended up in another backyard but the bird was nowhere to be found.

Then, as they dispiritedly stood talking, deciding that they had lost her, someone heard a slight noise behind them in the bushes. And there she was. They pounced, the bag was whisked off, and three happy young men watched as the lovely blue heron flew away to freedom.

I loved the story, but couldn't help thinking that many birds and animals must be caught in similar, horrible circumstances as a result of human carelessness. So when you see a plastic bag whizzing down the street, you might like to join me in pursuit.

It gives a new meaning to the term "baglady."

LISTEN TO THE CANARIES

Just before Christmas, 1989, Memorial University presented the fifth annual David Alexander lecture. Dr. Alexander was a highly respected and much beloved member of the History Department until his untimely death in 1980. He was a firm believer in the responsibility of universities to provide an informed critique of society.

The speaker for the lecture that year was a most appropriate choice: David Suzuki, world renowned scientist and communicator, whose topic was "Toward the year 2000." The message was not a happy one. It couldn't be, because he was describing the terrible environmental mess we are making of our planet.

Dr. Suzuki was just back from five weeks in Brazil where land-hungry developers are cutting down their magnificent Amazon rain forest at an alarming rate, just as we are doing in the equally magnificent forest in British Columbia. He pointed out the grave consequences for not only the people living in immediate areas but for the entire world.

The devastation in Brazil is an especially dramatic case, but everywhere the same processes are going on. Dr. Suzuki told the audience that within twenty or thirty years none of the world's great wilderness areas will be left. He described taking his two children to the Toronto zoo and the sadness he felt when his little girl would ask "Are there lots of these animals, Daddy?" He had to reply about one animal after another, "No, they are becoming extinct." Soon, he said, "The only rhinoceros will be those found in zoos. We are depleting our animal and plant life at the rate of two species an hour."

The arrogance of the human race is that we think we are somehow separate from nature instead of just being another species. Suzuki spoke of how we train children to go "yuk!" when they see a spider or bug, instead of teaching them to respect our interconnectedness with all living things. And, because we see ourselves as separate, we have been able to calmly destroy—with chemicals and other means—animal and plant life that is vital to our very being.

Concern about rain forests and rhinos is not just romantic nostalgia. We are all part of the same planetary system, and we need each other to survive. Dr. Suzuki reminded us that, in the old days, coal miners used to take canaries in cages down the mines with them. When the canaries died, the miners knew that their own lives were in danger. Those species that are disappearing every hour are our global canaries, and we are all in serious danger.

A major problem, Suzuki said, is our unquestioning belief in what officialdom calls growth. If the economy does not "grow," business people and economists call it a recession. But growth is using up resources and poisoning the environment at an ever-increasing rate. He was asked for his opinion on nuclear energy and replied that no ecologically aware scientist could recommend a system that has no proper ending. Quite apart from the explosive terrors of a Chernobyl, there is no method of safe disposal of waste products. The radioactivity lives on for hundreds and thousands of years. He scoffed at the suggestion that there was an oil glut, asking how it could be possible to have a glut of a non-renewable resource. Oil is finite and too precious a resource to be burned. We have to develop alternative energies, and we must go beyond the idea of zero-growth to an active policy of negative growth.

A student in the audience blamed the stupidity of elected politicians, but Suzuki countered with, "You're too young to be cynical. I have great respect for anyone who runs for parliament." But 70 percent of our legislators are business people and lawyers, and those groups are among the most ignorant of scientific matters. A young woman asked if that meant we should elect scientists, but he dismissed that idea. What is needed is for us all to become scientifically aware. When another student questioned what a concerned person could do, Dr. Suzuki answered with refreshing frankness that he didn't know, exactly. Each one should do what they felt would help—by joining the peace movement, the ecology movement, the search for alternate energy or whatever. It is irresponsible for any one of us—and particularly parents—not to be a part of the solution.

It was famed anthropologist Margaret Mead who said, "Never doubt that a small group of thoughtful, committed citizens can change the world. Indeed, it is the only thing that ever has."

That reminds me of a statement by Archbishop Desmond Tutu, on how to tackle problems that seem so overwhelming: "People often say oh, this problem is so big! And they shrug their shoulders with despair. They forget that there is only one way of eating an elephant—just taking one piece at a time."

Come to think of it, I suppose a simile about eating elephants is not entirely appropriate here, but you know what I mean. The important thing is that over 500 students, who had lined up for over an hour to get in, asked spirited questions and showed by their enthusiastic ovations that Dr. Suzuki had touched them deeply. David Alexander would have asked for no greater honour.

OUTRAGEOUS MISCONDUCT

Asbestos. The word comes from the Greek. Its usefulness has been known since the days of ancient Rome. And so have its dangers. The Roman naturalist, Pliny the Elder, observed that slaves developed sickness in the lungs when they wove asbestos into cloth.

Close to two thousand years later, industries were still being allowed to use asbestos in classrooms and homes and buildings even though industries and governments knew it to be carcinogenic. Laws were lax in protecting workers as well as the public. The people in Baie Verte can tell you of their struggle to get minimum safety precautions.

Their demands were pretty simple, but it took a strike before the company had to cover the mountains of tailings that blew asbestos dust over the town; before there were showers and changing rooms so that workers no longer had to take asbestos dust home to their families. A lot of St. John's people heard their appeals and stood on street corners shaking tin cans for donations to help the miners-on-strike and their families in Baie Verte.

Not long after that, *The New Yorker* ran a series of four articles by reporter Paul Brodeur who had studied the asbestos industry for twenty years. The articles became the basis of his book, *Outrageous Misconduct, The Asbestos Industry on Trial*, published by Pantheon Books in New York in 1985. It's a sorry tale of 50 years of cover-up by the asbestos industry and their friends in government. While industries were making their billions, hundreds of thousands of people were condemned to death by asbestos-induced cancer and related diseases.

The Johns-Manville Corporation was one of the wealthier companies, ranking 181 on the Fortune 500 scale of global wealth. With assets over two billion dollars in 1982, it was the most financially healthy company ever to go bankrupt. It did so to avoid the damage suits the company expected when the extent of the problem became known. The action was effective temporarily in stopping 17,000 product-liability lawsuits brought by victims. It took away the ability of juries to award punitive damages against Johns-Manville for "outrageous and reckless misconduct."

Brodeur's book tells how a handful of dedicated trial lawyers changed that. They pieced together the overwhelming evidence of the industry's cover-up, and won for their clients hundreds of millions of dollars in damage settlements.

Meanwhile people are still dying, and the industry is desperately looking for places where it can bury its deadly asbestos wastes which poison the water, the ground and the air we breathe.

Can our government be so outrageous and reckless that it would seriously offer Newfoundland as the toxic dumpsite of North America, the Maquiladora of the Atlantic? Many industries have tried to dump their deadly garbage on country after country. The world knows of our vast unemployment and sees us as a third-world country that can be pressured to accept a Bhopal, a Chernobyl or the pollution of our land and rivers as in the Mexican border area. Is this the level playing field advocated so happily by free trade adherents?

If our government doesn't stand strongly opposed to any importation of any kind of garbage, the message will go out that we're vulnerable. If we'll accept one sort of garbage, well, why not another? Who would sort through the mounds of any garbage to determine the contents? PCBs? Radioactive wastes? Missing bodies? It would all be buried in the thousands of pounds of garbage the barges from New York would be so happy to deposit on our soil and out of their state. Sure, there's lots of money in garbage, as has been said before, if you're willing to put people's lives at stake in the process.

Fortunately, there are people who are not willing to take such risks. A group of concerned citizens pressured the Newfoundland government to *Say No to American Garbage* (SNAG). The proposal to bring in asbestos tailings from the U.S. to Baie Verte seems to have died away. And so has the notion of barges of garbage from New York City. For the time being anyway.

A BEDTIME STORY

Now then, are you all snuggled down and ready for story time? All right. What sort of story would you like tonight? One about the old days? Well, let's see...

This story starts in a tiny village far, far away in a land of snow and ice, way back in 1988. It's a story about three whales who got into trouble, and a lot of people who tried to help them.

Somehow these three whales got trapped in miles and miles of ice. They had only a small hole where they could come up to breathe, and they couldn't swim away to be with the other whales. They couldn't find anything to eat, and after a while they got very hungry.

When reporters found out about it, they flew in from all over the world to take pictures and write things for newspapers and television. It was what they used to call a human interest story. It was also what they called a great photo opportunity. The reporters knew people would watch their pictures and read their stories, because they knew that most people are kind, and love animals, and care about things like freedom.

Besides, the reporters thought the story about the whales might take people's minds off other things that were going on, like elections and wars and things.

You see, in those days the whole world was divided into groups of people who thought other people were their enemies. Their governments spent a lot of time and money telling them how awful other people were. Two really big countries worked very hard at this kind of thing. Between them, they already controlled a big part of the world.

I know it's not easy for you to think about people being so mean, but back in those times grown-ups often did things just for money, or so they could control other people. Even bad, wicked things. Now we call it the Silly Period.

They knew how to build all sorts of wonderful machines that could do all sorts of wonderful things, but mostly they used them in ways that hurt people. They built bombs and submarines and rockets. And the things they built made poisons that got into the air and the water and the food. There were poisons in the grass that the cows ate, and in the milk that children drank. People were getting sick and dying, but the people who made the machines didn't seem to care. They went right on doing it.

In some places people didn't have enough to eat. Even little children died of hunger, while in other places people had so much to eat that they got sick and died from that.

Sometimes countries that had a lot of food would send some to countries that didn't have any, but it was never enough. Sometimes—quite often before an election—the governments of the big countries would talk about getting rid of the bombs and rockets but they never did. A lot of people were very worried. They held marches and demonstrations to try to get their government to change things, but nothing seemed to work.

So you can see why the reporters wanted to tell the story about the whales. They thought it might give people something different to think about for a change.

As soon as people heard about the whales, they wanted to help. One of the big countries that was making all the bombs and things sent out scientists and people who knew about ice and whales. The other big country that was also making bombs sent out its own scientists and was allowed to bring in its big ship that could cut through the ice. To their surprise, the scientists of both countries found that they didn't know as much about ice and whales as the native people who lived there.

And so the reporters told a story about two of the biggest and richest countries in the world, who spent most of their time making weapons to fight each other, co-operating with each other and a little group of people who didn't have bombs or rockets, who didn't want to fight anybody. The whole world watched on television while one of the native people smiled and waved and held up the flags of the two big countries, side by side.

And when the whales were finally set free, the whole world saw how easy it was for people to work together. They saw that other people didn't have to be their enemies. They realized that they didn't have to keep building weapons and poisoning the world but could begin to use their knowledge and machines to fight against hunger and sickness instead.

They realized that nobody had asked whether the whales were male or female, or what colour or age they were. They just wanted them to be free to swim in the ocean together, and have enough to eat, and be happy. And they realized that was what they really wanted for people, too.

So the big countries got together to help the poor countries just the way they helped the whales. Mothers and fathers laughed and clapped their hands because they knew their children could grow up in a world without starvation and hatred and war. When the whales were set free everybody was set free. And everybody lived happily ever after.

What's that you say, dear? Is it a true story? Well...parts of it are. Now a goodnight kiss and off to sleep.

SOME PUBLICATIONS AND ORGANIZATIONS I HAVE QUOTED OR MENTIONED

Publications:

Brodeur, Paul
1985 *Outrageous Misconduct*, New York: Pantheon

McQuaig, Linda
1988 *Behind Closed Doors*, Markham: Penguin
1991 *The Quick and the Dead*, Toronto: Penguin
1993 *The Wealthy Banker's Wife*, Toronto: Penguin
1995 *Shooting The Hippo*, Toronto:Penguin

O'Brien, Dereck
1991 *Suffer Little Children*, St. John's: Breakwater

Waring, Marilyn
1988 *If Women Counted*, San Francisco: Harper and Row

Kome, Penney
1983 *Play From Strength*, Ottawa: Canadian Advisory Council on the Status of Women

Barlow, Maude
and Campbell, Bruce
1990 *Parcel of Rogues*, Toronto: Key Porter
1991 *Take Back the Nation*, Toronto: Key Porter
1995 *Straight Through the Heart*, Toronto: Harper Collins

Barlow, Maude
and Heather-Jane Robertson,
1994 *Class Warfare*, Toronto: Key Porter

Finn, Ed
1995 *Monitor* Vol. 2, No. 6. (November), Ottawa: Canadian Centre for Policy Alternatives.

Brooks, Neil
1995 *Left vs. Right* Ottawa: Canadian Centre for Policy Alternatives.

McDonald, Marci
1995 *Yankee Doodle Dandy: Brian Mulroney and the American Agenda*. Toronto: Stoddart.

Organizations:
Council of Canadians
904-251 Laurier Ave. W., Ottawa, Ontario K1P 5J6
1-800-387-7177 or fax (613) 233-6776

Women's Network on Health and the Environment,
Connections (Newsletter)
c/o The Weed Foundation
736 Bathurst Street,
Toronto, ON, M5S 2R4
(416) 516-2600 or fax (416) 531-6214

Rachel's Hazardous Waste News
Environmental Research Foundation
P.O. Box 5036
Annapolis, MD 21403-7036

Canadian Centre for Policy Alternatives
#804-251 Laurier Ave. W., Ottawa, Ontario K1P 5J6

Canadian Forum (Canada's Leading Magazine on Politics and the Arts)
5502 Atlantic Street,
Halifax, NS B3H 9Z9